TOIL AND TROUBLE.

by Roland Müller

It's a spicy soup, and a heady brew at that. No recipe book can tell you how to make it. The ingredients are not on any supermarket shelves. A lot of people find it inedible. But then they want to indulge themselves despite everything: people are innovative, after all. Open to new ideas. Not narrow-minded. So: bon appétit! But even while you're sitting down at the table to enjoy this primal brew the cooks will have started experimenting with new versions of the recipe, and then that too will …

Taking the design scene's temperature.

Three years after Los Logos, the ultimate visual encyclopaedia of contemporary logo design, still not assimilated by the mainstream, and along comes the follow-up: Dos Logos. Like its predecessor, Dos Logos also illuminates the international design scene, again focusing on the current stage of development. It is working in real time, no flashbacks to old stories of commercial creations, heaped with re-wards, no presentations of trendy hot-shots, no signs that the whole world has already seen, and perhaps now started to ignore, no bor-ing repetitions: nothing that has already happened, but what is hap-pening NOW. What drives today's designers mad, and what drives them ahead? What inspires, motivates, demotivates them? How do they integrate current ideas and their personal perception of what's happening in the world and to things into their visual language: do they respond aggressively, ironically? Do they create harmonious counter-worlds, do they withdraw to secure positions and icons? How do they anticipate frequently contradictory ideas, requests and demands from their different partners and clients? What symbols or codes do they use in their work in order to make different functionalities in time and space visible and tangible in the logo? And what finally emerges from this "primal soup"? What does it look like – in terms of aesthetics, im-plementation and application? What does it provide – in the way of in-spiration? That's what Dos Logos is about. The spring is exciting – not the enormous, turgid river.

What thematic context do signs appear in?

The two Logos books differ in a few crucial points: Los Logos took four categories, signs, typograms, typefaces and combinations to ex-amine their formal quality from an expert and aesthetic point of view. This was done neutrally, not as an evaluation. Visual language, the art of creating form, handling fonts and other creative resources were central to the approach.

Dos Logos takes a step further and allows recipients to consider each logos within a thematic context and to see whether it interprets and represents. The structure of the book means that these additional views, comparison possibilities and judgment criteria fall into 10 themed chapters. The Los Logos categories – signs, typograms, typefaces, combinations – are retained and marked on each page to make navigation simpler (see caption on page 019). But mainly they are fulfilling a primary ordering function within the themed chap-ters listed below, which give the new structure a shape:

The new logo compendium also is different because it presents more extraordinary applications, places the logo, perhaps in a some-what fundamentalist way, in its cultural and social context, and tries to bridge the gap between pragmatic, functional signs and related signs in art.

Dos Logos brings together about 2800 signs from 24 countries. Dos Logos also provides information about the "makers" personal approach: a dozen designers from all over the world are interviewed briefly and make sharply focused statements on what a good logo is for them, where they draw their inspiration and how they handle their clients.

<u>The signified as a siren</u>

How can the broader view that DosLogos offers be defined and analysed, and what about the multiple planes of interpretation and possible readings? Why is it that the 10 thematically separate chapters can increase the recipients' insights? What is the concept?

According to Ferdinand de Saussure's linguistic paradigm, later developed further, reinterpreted and deconstructed by Roland Barthes, Umberto Eco and others, a sign consists of a signifier and a signified. Each sign is made up of two components: its meaning (signified) and its expressive side (signifier). The thing signified is outside this – it is interpreted by the sign, presented or also iconised.

Applied to the "Logo" as a sign, and to the book Dos Logos, this means: recipients can look at and assess the formal implementation, the aesthetic value of a logo (signifier = the expressive side) within a themed chapter, but they can also – by comparing with other logos interpreting the same theme, they can also find out something about what they mean (signified = the meaning), which opens up new possibilities for evaluating and comparing to readers.

Roland Barthes asserts that "the signifier is a siren". Though he doesn't mean the sort of siren that wails to warn us about a threatening catastrophe or an air raid, but the other kind: the seductive fabulous creature from Greek mythology that turns people's heads.

LOGOS ARE THE WORLD IN COMPRESSED FORM.

If it's true to say there is a logo or some other sign for almost anything and everything in our world, you could probably draw the following conclusion: signs present the whole world in compressed form. Every illustration is a designer's personal interpretation of the thing it stands for. So various sets of information can be found in a medium that brings current creations from the young designer scene together: firstly about the states of mind, attitudes, aesthetic trends and professional strategies of the designers themselves. But also about the current state of the world in general.

The world in compressed form. Is that a tenable thesis? Terry Eagleton, for example, says that any propaganda and popularisation requires making the complex simple. Swapping the word "logo" for "propaganda" and "popularisation" takes us straight to our subject. And then we immediately come across Eagleton's apparent paradox. He asserts that a transformation of this kind must involve deconstruction. His reason: if something complex can be turned into something simple, it cannot be as complex as it seems at a first glance … This could be applied to a designer's approach to a logo project: the complexity of a watch firm, a record label or a pizza baker can be contained if you abandon all the ballast, remove everything unimportant and concentrate on the essentials. Terry Eagleton goes on to say

[1] In other words, and this is relevant to our subject: the logo as an 'appropriate medium' is not so simple – because it has to be simple to read. And this is where the actual complexity is concealed.

The second part of the thesis remains: the current condition of the world. Designers draw inspiration from the world they live in. Where else could it come from, they do not know of any other! Current trends and tendencies, nature and technology, sport, arts and media, social developments on all planes and in all spheres, everything that happens – these are the sources they draw on according to their aesthetic ideas and preferences, and then include them in their creative work as appropriate to the project. And because designers are sensitive observers – they actually have to be – they reflect, because it is their raw material, everything they see, hear, sense and feel, that they love and hate in their work. And so they also reflect the variety of the world as it presently is and – perhaps also – how it could or should be. In other words: signs do not just define the object they were created for, but in their own way they also help to define the world as such.

My logo is my castle

insists Gerhard Richter in a discussion of his work WAR CUT.[2] This is an attitude shared by many designers concerned with creating logos and other signs. Transitions have become fluid anyway, and all sorts of interactions take place between so-called "pure art" and "pragmatic" design. Not least in the signs' own territory.

But what does form look like, how does it manifest itself - arising as it quite often does from the wreckage of obsolete forms - when it confronts facts on today's logo design scene? This is boom time for short-lived zeitgeist exponents.

Pretty little Mangas, still among the darlings of the scene, are still clinging on, but they are on their way out. Sayonara! Love & Peace have not brought geo-political harmony, but there are still some people determined to keep the rainbow flag up to scratch. And on a related but rather more aggressive side of the same spectrum, actual losers of wars and alleged winners of wars are appearing on logos. But their days of relevancy are numbered. Something that is interesting for the uninvolved observer, but probably giving food for

thought in the ranks of the cultural historians, is using 'beautiful' quotations.

says Dirk Baecker[3] in an essay. And sometimes the beautiful can be a logo of a beautiful logo. It is not the Greek goddess of victory who is being cited, but the world-wide, omnipresent sign citing her. But this has nothing to do with Postmodern sampling. That was the day before yesterday. Ultimately the new love of heraldry is striking. Perhaps it is trying to tell us that roadholding is in fashion again. We are in times of new imponderables, and a new trend towards curling up in a ball and barricading ourselves up is gaining ground. Not an optimistic view. But perhaps it is all just about ironic quotations of glory and splendour.

But sometimes these somewhat martial-seeming coats-of-arms are providing information about something else, something very up to date. And that is about the consequences that the latent "momentariness" of our society is imposing on our logos: my logo is my castle. Nothing that is happening can last for ever. The presence of a new logo least of all. It has to be loud, it has to be strong and it has to be today. Strong as a fortress towering over the steep valley and dominating the entire landscape. Not a little house in the country, not a rose garden. But, and this is the point: when building a castle we use the most solid, the most resistant materials, but it does not stand for long. In a few years, perhaps even earlier, it will be pulled down again and promptly replaced by a new one.

It is quite clear that by building these castles, which are no more than powerful identities, we are just using crude devices and loud noises to resist the omnipresent massive overstimulation to a certain extent. The castle's chance of being acknowledged is considerably greater than that of a discreetly emerging sign. Signifier (expression) comes before signified (meaning). The degree of expression is so

strongly accented, so aetheticised, that it can function, has to function and will function only in the NOW time window. Of course there
is some level of differentiation, corporate logos do not attack recipients in a wild fashion. But the general trend cannot be overlooked
there either, even if it is a little more contained, tempered.

Ten sectors to look at

Headlines in the lifestyle press always promise "all about ..."
when they announce a theme. This is not what Dos Logos is trying to
do. Ten sectors are briefly introduced here, intended to offer no more,
and also no less, than a representative cross-section, a snapshot of
current logo design practice.

Seriousness is once again the order of the day in the Corporate
chapter. But it is precisely this that makes projects from this sphere
particularly interesting for designers. Numerous examples show how
tension between the designer's and the client's and his brand's identity can lead to appealing solutions. One important aspect of this sec-
tor is the multifunctionality of the logo, which has to work in all applications. A visiting card is like a lorry.

The Culture chapter is distinguished by strong signs. Not really
radical, but fairly experimental. The designers' affinity with art and
culture can be clearly felt. Typical exponents are playful, charming, but
also cheeky and absurd figures, with hints of old and everyday myths.

The Design chapter is of course about bold self-representation.
Here designers are seeking to make an impact, and their courage –
and sometimes their lack of inhibition as well – knows no bounds.
They strike wild and ironic attitudes, set the signs a-dancing and also
force recipients to address some unintelligible typefaces. Attracting
attention is just as important as being attractive. Or even more important, and there is a particularly broad experimental field open to
heraldry here.

Design in the Fashion chapter adopts an aesthetically beautiful
formal language. The motifs are markedly bold and eye-catching.
Fabulous creatures in attractive frames grind their teeth, signs are
imitated, off-beat slogans brought into play, ornamental typefaces
used, and heraldry is en vogue, partly because it looks so good on
T-shirts.

The in Motion and Games chapter. The little pictograms and illustrative figures don't have to be charming here, they can be cheeky
and absurd as well. Sometimes even kung-fu warriors. The motion
section demonstrates the development of logos – in movement, and
in building up towards a definitive form.

It's some time since Marshall McLuhan told us that "the medium
is the message". This is somehow still true, even though conditions
have changed completely, and the designers in the Media chapter in-
evitably are and remain focused on the character of the particular
medium. A new mag for a trendy target group follows quite different
rules from those for an opinion-forming daily or a sober newsletter.
Jolly little icons that love cavorting on the Net bring some colourful
variety on to the scene.

Nothing changes as quickly as the music scene. Rapid transfor-
mations are its only constant. This is why designs in the Music chapter feature the most markedly visual sound. Music styles define themselves in clichés. This makes them easily recognisable. And today's
music trend is replaced tomorrow. This opens up creative perspec-
tives that are fully exploited and also sometimes overused.

Political and Social. The contrast could not be greater. You could
almost talk about warring opposites. A hot political campaign has to
be approached differently from a social institution or the German Par-
liament ...! A nice, refined little logo for a charity organisation along-
side "nine-eleven" as a theme for a political protest event.

Art and unclassifiable Signs. Olaf Nicolai, an artist whose actual
theme is bringing all spheres of life together, also creates logos. But

not for the brand he is promoting, and also not in their original size either, but blown up to monstrous proportions. The interfaces between pragmatic, functional and free "purposeless" signs are evident, they are exciting and make you think, which is entirely appropriate to their intentions. Delight in experimentation, pleasure in provocation are expressed here in a whole range of ways. But the mainstream is looking on, and a lot of things that are lording it on the art pedestal today will be on the streets tomorrow.

It's no good looking for big names in the Sport chapter: no design experiments for the big sports goods manufacturers! The picture is similar for sporting disciplines. So it is mainly the young, trendy sports that have not yet been taken over by Big Business like snowboarding or skateboarding that feature in this chapter, complemented by small labels that are trying to make a name for themselves on the scene with unusual and imaginative signs.

Designers are not chameleons

Designers become known to potential clients and other interested parties, for example the media or the art scene, through the character, style and quality of their work – their signs, for example. And by being professional designers, they are demonstrating a very definite, self-defined creative approach.

Essentially something that is taken for granted. But there is a problem: choosing the right strategy.

Let us assume that Designer X introduces a very high proportion of his own identity into his work. He thinks that's quite normal, it's part of the way he sees himself and is something that can also be called a professional ethos – even though that sounds somewhat old-fashioned. But the client perhaps does not see it like that, and demands an identity for his brand. Their professional association could well come to an end.

Designer Y chooses the opposite strategy. He is far more (perhaps too) reticent. He behaves as neutrally as possible, because for him the highest priority is the best possible solution for the client (best possible from the client's point of view). And so where necessary he is prepared to make aesthetic compromises. Here too the client could react negatively. In his opinion the logo embodies his Corporate Strategy. But he misses what he calls a "creative kick". Their professional association could well come to an end.

But clients also pursue a variety of strategies. So there is a perfectly realistic scenario whereby Designer X is confirmed in his approach: at the point where the client wants to participate in the designer's identity and communicate it to his clients. (Comparisons can be a little lame, but why does an anonymous department store pep up its fabrics with a known fashion designer's label?)

These scenarios quite deliberately present opposing positions to highlight the conflict potential a designer can be confronted with. This potential tends to be even greater in economically difficult times. In daily practice, a mixture of Designer X's and Designer Y's strategy should make sense from case to case, because it is pragmatic. But one thing is certain: a marked sense of optimism in dealing with clients is a career killer in the long term. A designer who adapts too much can never develop his own pictorial language – and so will not acquire a profile as a designer, will not have an identity of his own. And this is a fatal disadvantage when looking for new business.

1.   Neue Zürcher Zeitung, 29./30.5.2004
2.   Quotation from: www.newsmuseum.org/now_cur_diez.php
3.   Dirk Baecker, "Etwas Theorie", www.uni-wh.de/baecker

010

DIE URSUPPE IST ANGERICHTET.

von Roland Müller

Sie ist stark gewürzt und sehr aromatisch. Ihre Zubereitungsart steht in keinem Rezeptbuch. Ihre Ingredienzen fehlen im Regal des Supermarktes. Manchen scheint sie ungenießbar. Aber daran laben wollen sich irgendwie trotzdem alle: Man ist schließlich innovativ. Neuem gegenüber aufgeschlossen. Und kein Banause. Also dann: Bon appetit! Doch während man sich zu Tisch begibt, um sich die Ursuppe schmecken zu lassen, werden die Köche schon längst wieder am Ausprobieren neuer Rezepte sein, die dann wiederum...

Das Befindlichkeits-Thermometer der Gestalterszene.

Drei Jahre nach Los Logos, der ultimativen visuellen Enzyklopädie des zeitgemäßen, noch nicht vom Mainstream vereinnahmten Logo-Designs, liegt nun das Follow-Up vor: Dos Logos. Wie sein Vorgänger leuchtet auch Dos Logos die internationale Gestalterszene aus, wobei der Fokus wiederum auf dem ganz aktuellen Entwicklungsstand liegt, der Echtzeit: Keine Rückblenden auf alte Geschichten kommerziell erfolgreicher, mit Awards überhäufter Kreationen, keine Präsentation arrivierter Top-Shots, keine Zeichen, die schon von der ganzen Welt gesehen wurden und vielleicht schon längst übersehen werden, keine langweiligen Repetitionen; nichts, was bereits passiert ist, sondern das, was gerade JETZT passiert. Was treibt den Designer heute um, und was treibt ihn an? Was inspiriert, motiviert, demotiviert ihn? Auf welche Art lässt er die Aktualität und seine persönliche Wahrnehmung des Laufes der Welt und der Dinge in seine visuelle Sprache einfließen: Reagiert er aggressiv, ironisch? Schafft er harmonische Gegenwelten, zieht er sich auf sichere Positionen und Ikonen zurück? Wie antizipiert er die oftmals konträren Vorstellungen, Wünsche und Anforderungen seiner unterschiedlichen Partner, Kunden und Auftraggeber? Welche Chiffren oder Codes setzt er bei seiner Arbeit ein, um differierende Funktionalitäten in Raum und Zeit im Logo sicht- und nacherlebbar zu machen? Und was entsteht schließlich aus dieser „Ursuppe": Wie sieht das aus – in der Ästhetik, der Umsetzung und den Applikationen? Was gibt das her – an Inspirationen? Darum geht es in Dos Logos. Nicht der große träge Strom ist spannend, sondern die sprudelnde Quelle.

In welchem thematischen Kontext erscheint das Zeichen?

In einigen wesentlichen Punkten unterscheiden sich die beiden Logos-Bände: Los Logos untersucht in den vier Kategorien Zeichen, Typogramme, Schriftzüge und Kombinationen primär deren formale Qualität aus einem fachlich-ästhetischen Blickwinkel. Dies geschieht auf neutrale, nicht wertende Weise. Die visuelle Sprache, die Kunst der Formgebung, der Umgang mit Fonts und anderen Gestaltungsmitteln stehen im Zentrum der Betrachtungsweise.

Dos Logos geht nun noch einen Schritt weiter und erlaubt es den RezipientInnen, jedes Logo innerhalb des Themas zu betrachten und zu vergleichen, das es interpretiert und repräsentiert. Diese zusätzlichen Sichtweisen, Vergleichsmöglichkeiten und Beurteilungskriterien ergeben sich durch die Gliederung des Buches in zehn thematische Kapitel. Die Kategorien von Los Logos – Zeichen, Typogramme, Schriftzüge, Kombinationen – werden beibehalten und zur einfacheren Navigation zusätzlich auf sämtlichen Seiten markiert (siehe Legende auf Seite 019). Doch sie erfüllen primär eine formale Ordnungsfunktion innerhalb der im Folgenden aufgeführten thematischen Kapitel, die der neuen Struktur Gestalt geben:

Darüber hinaus unterscheidet sich das neue Logo-Kompendium durch eine vermehrte Präsentation außergewöhnlicher Applikationen, stellt das Logo als Zeichen in seinen kulturellen und gesellschaftlichen Kontext und versucht einen Brückenschlag von den pragmatischen, zweckorientierten Zeichen zu verwandten Zeichen in der Kunst.

Die in Dos Logos versammelten, etwa 2800 Zeichen stammen aus 24 Ländern. Was die persönliche Haltung der „Macher" angeht, so gibt Dos Logos auch darüber Auskunft: In kurzen Interviews verraten ein Dutzend Designer aus aller Welt in sehr pointierten Aussagen, was für sie ein gutes Logo ist, woher sie ihre Inspirationen beziehen und wie sie mit ihren Auftraggebern umgehen.

<u>Der Signifikant ist eine Sirene.</u>

Wie lässt sich die erweiterte Sichtweise, wie lassen sich die multiplen Leseebenen und Interpretationsmöglichkeiten definieren und transparent machen, die DosLogos anbietet? Warum generieren die zehn thematisch abgegrenzten Kapitel Erkenntnisgewinne für die RezipientInnen? Was ist das Konzept?

Nach Ferdinand de Saussures linguistischem Paradigma, das später von Roland Barthes, Umberto Eco und anderen weiterentwickelt, uminterpretiert und auch dekonstruiert wurde, setzt sich das Zeichen aus einer Bezeichnung und einem Bezeichneten zusammen. Jedes Zeichen besteht aus zwei Komponenten: seiner Bedeutungsseite (Signifikat) und seiner Ausdrucksseite (Signifikant). Die bezeichnete Sache selbst liegt außerhalb – sie wird vom Zeichen interpretiert, dargestellt oder auch ikonisiert.

Auf das Zeichen „Logo" und das Buch Dos Logos angewandt bedeutet dies: Die RezipientInnen haben die Möglichkeit, innerhalb eines thematischen Kapitels nicht nur die formale Umsetzung, den ästhetischen Wert eines Logos (Signifikant = die Ausdruckseite) zu betrachten und zu beurteilen, sondern sie können – im Vergleich mit anderen, die gleiche Thematik interpretierenden Logos – auch etwas über seine Bedeutung (Signifikat = die Bedeutung) erfahren, was ihnen neue Wertungs- und Vergleichsmöglichkeiten erschließt.

„Der Signifikant ist eine Sirene", behauptet Roland Barthes. Womit er nicht jene meint, die bei einer drohenden Katastrophe oder einem Bomberangriff losheult, sondern die andere: das verführerische Fabelwesen aus der griechischen Mythologie, das den Leuten den Kopf verdrehte.

LOGOS SIND DIE WELT
IN KOMPRIMIERTER GESTALT.

Wenn in unserer Welt für fast alles und jedes ein Logo oder anderes Zeichen steht, dann könnte man als These folgende Schlußfolgerung ableiten: Zeichen bilden die ganze Welt in komprimierter Form ab. Jede Abbildung ist eine persönliche Interpretation des Designers von der Sache, für die sie steht. Also lassen sich in einem Medium, in dem sich die aktuellsten Kreationen der jungen Designerszene versammeln, verschiedene Auskünfte einholen: einmal über die Befindlichkeiten, Einstellungen, ästhetischen Trends und professionellen Strategien der Gestalter selbst, zum Anderen aber auch über den aktuellen Zustand der Welt ganz generell.

Die Welt in komprimierter Gestalt: Ist das eine haltbare These? Terry Eagleton zum Beispiel sagt, dass jede Propaganda und Popularisierung die Umwandlung des Komplexen ins Einfache verlangt. Ein Austausch der Begriffe „Propaganda" und „Popularisierung" durch „Logo" führt direkt zurück zum Thema. Und jetzt kommt das scheinbare Eageton'sche Paradox. Er behauptet nämlich, dass eine solche Umwandlung absolut dekonstruktivistisch sei. Seine Begründung: Wenn sich etwas Komplexes in etwas Einfaches umwandeln lässt, dann kann es gar nicht so komplex sein, wie es auf den ersten Blick erscheint... Das ließe sich auch auf die Herangehensweise des Designers an ein Logoauftragsprojekt übertragen: Die Komplexität einer Uhrenfirma, eines Plattenlabels oder eines Pizzabäckers halten sich in Grenzen, wenn man allen Ballast abwirft, alles Unwichtige abstrahiert und sich auf die „Essentials" konzentriert. Weiter im Text Terry Eagleton:

[1] Mit anderen, aufs Thema applizierten Worten: Das ‚adäquate Medium' Logo ist gar nicht so einfach – weil es einfach zu lesen sein muss. Darin versteckt sich die eigentliche Komplexität.

Bleibt der zweite Teil der These: Der aktuelle Weltzustand. Der Designer bezieht die Inspirationen für seine Arbeit aus der Welt, in der er lebt. Woher auch sonst, er kennt ja keine andere! Aktuelle Trends und Tendenzen, die Natur und die Technologie, der Sport, die Medien und die Kunst, die gesellschaftliche Entwicklung auf allen Ebenen und in allen Bereichen; alles, was passiert - das sind die Quellen, die er seinen ästhetischen Vorstellungen und Präferenzen gemäß ausschöpft und projektbezogen in seine gestalterische Arbeit einfließen lässt. Und weil Designer als sensible Beobachter - eigentlich zwangsläufig - alles, was sie sehen, hören, ahnen und fühlen, was sie lieben und hassen, als Rohmaterial für ihre Arbeit betrachten, widerspiegeln sie in ihrer Vielfalt die Welt, wie sie im aktuellen Zustand beschaffen ist, und – vielleicht auch – wie sie sein könnte oder sollte. Mit anderen Worten: Zeichen bezeichnen eben nicht nur den Gegenstand, für den sie kreiert wurden, sondern sind in ihrer Art auch ein wenig bezeichnend für die Welt an sich.

My Logo is my Castle.

betont Gerhard Richter in einem Gespräch über seine Arbeit WAR CUT. [2] Eine Haltung, die von vielen Designern, die sich mit der Gestaltung von Logos und anderen Zeichen beschäftigen, geteilt wird. Überhaupt sind ja die Übergänge fließend geworden, und zwischen der sogenannten „pur Art" und dem „pragmatischen" Design finden die vielfältigsten Interaktionen statt. Nicht zuletzt auf dem Gebiet der Zeichen selbst.

Doch wie sehen die Formen, die Ausformungen, mit denen den Fakten begegnet wird, und die nicht selten aus der Zertrümmerung obsoleter Formen hervorgehen, in der Szene der Logogestalter heute aus? Kurzlebige Zeitgeist-Exponenten haben Hochkonjunktur.

Die niedlichen Mangas, eben noch zu den Lieblingen der Szene gehörend, haben sich zwar nicht ganz verabschiedet, aber sie befinden sich auf dem Rückzug. Sayonnara! Love & Peace hat es zwar geopolitisch nicht gebracht, aber es gibt noch immer Unbeirrbare, die der Regenbogenflagge die Stange halten. Auf einer verwandten, aber doch eher aggressiven Seite des gleichen Spektrums machen sich tatsächliche Kriegsverlierer und angebliche Kriegsgewinnler auf Logos breit. Aber die Tage ihrer aktuellen Relevanz sind gezählt. Interessant für den neutralen Beobachter, aber in der Riege der Kulturkritiker wahrscheinlich einen neuen Nachdenklichkeitsschub auslösend, ist das Zitieren ‚schöner' Zitate.

wie Dirk Baecker [3] in einem Aufsatz meint. Und so ist dann manchmal das Schöne auch ein Logo von einem schönen Logo. Nicht die griechische Siegesgöttin wird zitiert, sondern das weltweit überpräsente Zeichen, das sie zitiert. Was aber keineswegs mit dem postmodernen Sampling zu verwechseln ist. Das war vorgestern. Schließlich fällt die neue Liebe zur Heraldik auf. Eventuell will sie uns sagen, dass Bodenhaftung wieder gefragt ist in Zeiten der Unabwägbarkeiten, dass eine neue Tendenz zum Einigeln und sich Verbarrikadieren an Boden gewinnt. Keine optimistische Vorstellung. Doch vielleicht geht es nur um ironische Zitate der Epoche von Glanz und Gloria.

Allerdings geben die gelegentlich etwas martialisch daher kommenden Wappen auch über etwas Anderes, sehr Zeitgemässes Auskunft. Nämlich über Konsequezen der latenten „Augenblicklichkeit" unserer Gesellschaft auf die Gestaltung von Logos: My Logo is my Castle. Nichts, was passiert, währt ewig. Die Präsenz eines neuen Logos schon gar nicht. Es muss laut, es muss stark, und es muss heute sein. Stark wie eine Trutzburg, die über dem tiefen Tal steht und die ganze Landschaft beherrscht. Kein Häuschen im Grünen, kein Rosengarten. Aber, und das ist der Punkt: Beim Bau der Burg kommen zwar die solidesten, widerstandsfähigsten Materialen zum Einsatz, aber sie bleibt nicht lange stehen. In wenigen Jahren, vielleicht sogar schon früher, wird sie wieder abgerissen und prompt durch eine neue ersetzt.

Der Bau dieser Burgen, die nichts anderes als markante Identitäten sind, ist klar: Mit krassen Mitteln und lauten Tönen lässt sich der allgegenwärtigen massiven Reizüberflutung etwas entgegen setzen, dessen Wahrnehmungschancen wesentlich grösser sind als diejenigen eines diskret auftretenden Zeichens. Signifikant (Ausdruck) kommt vor Signifikat (Bedeutung). Der Ausdrucksgrad wird so stark akzentuiert und ästhetisiert, dass es nur im Zeitfenster des JETZT funktionieren kann, funktionieren muss und funktionieren wird. Natürlich wird differenziert, fallen Logos für den Corporate-Bereich nicht wild über die Rezipienten her. Aber der allgemeine Trend, wenn auch etwas dosiert, temperiert, ist selbst dort nicht zu übersehen.

<u>Zehn Sektoren zur Besichtigung.</u>
„Alles über…", versprechen die Schlagzeilen der Lifestyle-Presse jeweils, wenn sie ein Thema ankündigen. Das ist nicht die Intention von Dos Logos. Nicht mehr, aber auch nicht weniger als ein repräsentativer Querschnitt, eine Momentaufnahme der aktuellen Logo-Gestaltungspraxis, wird in den nachfolgenden, kurz vorgestellten zehn Sektoren geboten.

Im Corporate-Kapitel ist nach wie vor Seriosität die Regel. Aber gerade das macht ein Projekt aus diesem Bereich zu einer besonders interessanten Herausforderung für den Gestalter. Zahlreiche Beispiele zeigen, wie aus dem Spannungsverhältnis zwischen der Identität des Desigerns und derjenigen des Kunden und seiner Marke ansprechende Lösungen entstehen können. Ein wichtiger Aspekt in diesem Sektor ist die Multifunktionalität des Logos, das in allen Anwendungen funktionieren muss. Eine Visitenkarte ist wie ein Lastwagen.

Starke Zeichen prägen das Kulturelle Kapitel. Nicht richtig radikal, aber ziemlich experimentell. Man spürt sie deutlich, die Affinität der Designer zu Kunst und Kultur. Verspielte, liebe, aber auch freche und skurrile Figuren mit Anklängen an alte und Alltagsmythen sind typische Exponenten.

Im Kapitel Design, wo es natürlich um krasse Selbstdarstellungen geht, mit denen man sich profilieren möchte, kennt der Mut – und gelegentlich auch die Unverfrorenheit – keine Grenzen. Man gebärdet sich wild und ironisch, lässt die Zeichen tanzen und mutet den Rezipienten auch unlesbare Schriften zu. Auffallen ist ebenso wichtig wie Gefallen. Oder sogar wichtiger, und für die Heraldik besteht hier ein breites Experimentierfeld.

Eine ästhetisch schöne Formsprache pflegt das Design im Kapitel Mode. Die Motive sind ausgesprochen plakativ. Fabelwesen in attraktiven Rahmen fletschen die Zähne, Zeichen werden imitiert, schräge Slogans apppliziert, ornamentale Schriften eingesetzt und Heraldik ist en vogue, auch weil sie so schön aufs T-Shirt passt.

In Motion und Games Kapitel. Die Piktogrämmchen und illustrativen Figürchen müssen nicht lieb, sie können auch frech und skurril sein. Manchmal sogar Kung Fu - kämpferisch. In der Abteilung Motion wird die Entwicklung von Logos demonstriert – in der Bewegung und im Aufbau bis zur definitiven Form.

„The Medium is the Message", hat schon der alte McLuhan gesagt. Das gilt unter völlig veränderten Bedingungen irgendwie noch immer, und die Designer im Kapitel Media sind und bleiben zwangsläufig auf den jeweiligen Mediencharakter fokussiert. Das neue Magazin für eine trendige Zielgruppe gehorcht eben anderen Gesetzen als die meinungsbildende Tageszeitung oder der nüchterne Newsletter. Bunte Abwechslung in die Szenerie bringen die lustigen kleinen Icons, die sich mit Vorliebe im Web tummeln.

Nichts verändert sich so schnell wie die Musikszene. Schnelle Wechsel sind ihre einzige Konstante. Deshalb zeigt das Design im

Kapitel Musik immer den angesagtesten visuellen Sound. Musikstile definieren sich über Klischees. Das generiert schnellen Wiedererkennungswert. Und die Musikrichtung von heute wird morgen abgelöst. Das eröffnet gestalterische Perspektiven, die voll ausgenutzt und auch mal überstrapaziert werden.

Das Kapitel Politik und Soziales: Größer könnten die Kontraste nicht sein. Man könnte fast von antagonistischen Gegensätzen sprechen. Attac muss anders angegangen werden als ein Sozialwerk oder der Deutsche Bundestag! Ein kleines, feines Logo für eine Wohltätigkeits-Organisation neben dem Thema „nine-eleven" für ein politisches Protest-Event.

Zum Kapitel Kunst und unklassierbare Zeichen. Olaf Nicolai, ein Künstler, dessen eigentliches Thema die Vereinnahmung aller Lebensbereiche ist, kreiert ebenfalls Logos. Aber nicht für die Marke, die er darin abbildet, und auch nicht in Originalgröße, sondern monsterhaft aufgeblasen. Die Schnittstellen zwischen pragmatischen, zweckorientierten und freien, „zwecklosen" Zeichen sind evident, sie sind spannend und stimmen nachdenklich, was ganz ihren Intentionen entspricht. Die Freude am Experimentieren, die Lust am Provozieren drückt sich hier auf vielfältigste Weise aus. Doch der Mainstream schaut auch zu, und manches, was heute auf dem Sockel der Kunst thront, begibt sich morgen auf die Straße.

Im Kapitel Sport sucht man vergebens nach den großen Namen: Keine Designexperimente bei den etablierten Sportartikelherstellern! Ähnliches Bild bei den sportlichen Disziplinen. Deshalb sind es vor allem die jungen, noch nicht vom Big Business vereinnahmten Trendsportarten wie Snowboarding oder Skateboarding, die man in diesem Kapitel antrifft, ergänzt von kleinen Labels, die sich mit ausgefallenen und fantasievollen Zeichen in der Szene profilieren möchten.

<u>Designer sind keine Chamäleons.</u>

Der Gestalter wird durch den Charakter, den Stil und die Qualität seiner Arbeit – zum Beispiel Zeichen – von potenziellen Kunden und anderen Interessenten – zum Beispiel Medien oder der Kunstszene – wahrgenommen. Und manifestiert als professioneller Designer mit seiner Tätigkeit eine ganz von ihm selbst definierte, bestimmte gestalterische Haltung.

Im Grunde genommen eine Selbstverständlichkeit. Doch es gibt ein Problem: Die Wahl der richtigen Strategie.

Einmal angenommen, Designer X bringt einen sehr hohen Anteil der eigenen Identität in seine Arbeiten ein. Er findet das auch ganz normal, es gehört zu seinem Selbstverständnis und ist etwas, das man auch Berufsethos nennen könnte – obwohl es etwas altmodisch klingt. Der Kunde sieht das aber vielleicht nicht ganz so und fordert die Identität seiner Marke ein. Ein mögliches Ende der Geschäftsbeziehung ist nicht auszuschließen.

Designer Y wählt die konträre Strategie: Er nimmt sich selbst (vielleicht zu sehr) zurück. Er verhält sich möglichst neutral, weil für ihn die bestmögliche Lösung für den Auftraggeber (bestmöglich aus Kundensicht) absolute Priorität hat. Dabei geht er, wenn's denn sein muss, auch schon einmal ästhetische Kompromisse ein. Auch hier könnte die Reaktion des Kunden negativ ausfallen. Das Logo verkörpert seiner Meinung nach die Corporate Strategy. Aber er vermisst das, was er als „kreativen Kick" bezeichnet. Ein mögliches Ende der Geschäftsbeziehung ist nicht auszuschließen.

Doch Auftraggeber verfolgen ebenfalls die unterschiedlichsten Strategien. Also ist auch ein Szenario durchaus realistisch, in dem Designer X in seiner Haltung bestätigt wird: Dann nämlich, wenn der Kunde an der Identität des Designers partizipieren und sie seinen Kunden kommunizieren möchte. (Vergleiche hinken zwar gewöhnlich, aber warum peppt wohl ein anonymes Kaufhaus seine Textilien mit dem Label eines angesagten Modedesigners auf?)

Diese Szenarien schildern ganz bewusst gegensätzliche Positionen, um das Konfliktpotenzial anschaulicher zu machen, mit dem der Designer konfrontiert werden kann. Ein Potenzial, das sich in wirtschaftlich schwierigeren Zeiten eher vergrößert. In der täglichen Praxis dürfte von Fall zu Fall ein Mix aus der Strategie des Designers X mit derjenigen des Designers Y sinnvoll, weil pragmatisch sein. Eines ist jedoch sicher: Ausgeprägter Opportunismus im Umgang mit den Kunden ist langfristig gesehen ein Karrierekiller. Ein Designer, der sich zu sehr anpasst, kann keine eigene Bildsprache entwickeln – und somit auch kein Profil als Designer, keine eigene Identität. Ein Nachteil mit fatalen Folgen bei der Akquise.

1.   Neue Zürcher Zeitung, 29./30.5.2004
2.   Zitat von: www.newsmuseum.org/now_cur_diez.php
3.   Dirk Baecker, „Etwas Theorie", www.uni-wh.de/baecker

Signs
abstract, pictographic, ikono-
graphic, ideographic, illustrative

Zeichen
abstrakt, piktografisch, ikonografisch, ideografisch, illustrativ

•

Typograms

Typogramme

Lettering

Schriftzüge

—

Vertical combinations
on top of / among
each other

Vertikale Kombinationen
über- / untereinander

Symmetrical combinations
centred

Symmetrische Kombinationen
zentriert

Horizontal combinations
sign + lettering
side by side

Horizontale Kombinationen
Zeichen + Schriftzug
nebeneinander

Horizontal combinations
lettering + sign
side by side

Horizontale Kombinationen
Schriftzug + Zeichen
neben einander

Complex combinations
fusion

Komplexe Kombinationen
Verschmelzungen

CORPORATE

What can young designers come up with when they are creatively challenged by the world of commerce, big and small businesses, banks and companies, hotels and restaurants, craftsmen and dealers? This chapter will show.

CORPORATE

Was haben die jungen Gestalter drauf, wenn sie von der Geschäftswelt, von Big und Small Business, von Banken und Unternehmen, Hotels und Restaurants, Handwerkern und Händlern kreativ herausgefordert werden? In diesem Kapitel wird es aufgezeigt.

BLEED

"THERE'S ALWAYS MORE THAN ONE SOLUTION."

Where do you get inspiration for your work?
From any aesthetic object, fashion and architecture, history and everything around us. Anything that triggers an emotion or conveys a feeling to you is inspiring.

Do you work according to a definite design philosophy?
Only design things we like ourselves. Be proud of our own work.

What would you say is the key to a good, successful logo?
A good logo should be easy to recognise and work whatever it's used for. A great logo never needs redesigning and makes you feel good.

Do your aesthetic values and your clients' demands ever clash?
There's always more than one solution. Once you've internalised that there shouldn't be any conflicts. It's all both a wide range of style and thought.

If a client wasn't prepared to accept your work, how far would you be prepared to compromise?
We are prepared to go as far as is useful for the project. If you've had a good dialogue with your client there shouldn't be any conflict, just co-operation. If the dialogue becomes a monologue there will be conflicts, and no co-operation.

Wo holt ihr euch die Inspirationen für eure Arbeit?
Von allen ästhetischen Objekten, Mode und Architektur, Geschichte und allem, was uns umgibt. Alles, was ein Gefühl auslöst oder dir ein Gefühl vermittelt, ist inspirierend.

Arbeitet ihr nach einer definierten Designphilosophie?
Immer nur Sachen gestalten, die uns selbst gefallen. Stolz sein auf die eigene Arbeit.

Was charakterisiert in euren Augen ein gutes, ein gelungenes Logo?
Ein gutes Logo sollte leicht erkennbar sein und funktional für jede Anwendung. Ein großes Logo braucht nie ein Redesign und gibt dir ein gutes Gefühl.

Gibt's Konflikte zwischen euren ästhetischen Wertvorstellungen und den Ansprüchen eurer Kunden?
Es gibt immer mehr als nur eine Lösung. Wenn man das verinnerlicht hat, sollte es keine Konflikte geben. Auf ein breites Spektrum im Stil und im Denken kommt es an.

Angenommen, ein Kunde akzeptiert eure Arbeit nicht: Wie weit lasst ihr euch dann auf Kompromisse ein?
Wir sind darauf eingestellt, so weit zu gehen, wie es dem Projekt nützt. Wenn du einen guten Dialog mit dem Kunden führst, sollte es keine Konflikte geben, sondern Kooperation. Falls der Dialog zum Monolog wird, gibt's Konflikte und wir beenden die Zusammenarbeit.

Bleed, Oslo, Norway | www.bleed.no

Bleed, Oslo, Norwegen | www.bleed.no

•

022.1 viagrafik

022.2 Binnenland

022.3 Kong

022.4 strange//attraktor

022.5 Kong

022.6 FUTRO

022.7 METHOD

022.8 strange//attraktor

022.9 Kong

022.10 Kong

022.11 hirschindustries

022.12 H5

023.1 Rinzen

023.2 Norm

023.3 Norm

023.4 studiotonne

023.5 canefantasma studio

023.6 FUTRO

023.7 METHOD

023.8 nothing medialab

023.9 METHOD

023.10 Nendo Graphic Squad

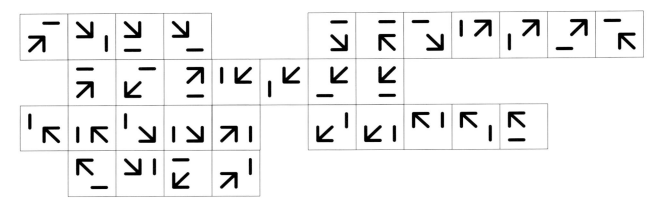

024.1 Norm

024.2 WG Berlin

024.3 WG Berlin

025.1 Gianni Rossi

025.2 Felix Braden

025.3 FUTRO

025.4 Felix Braden

025.5 FUTRO

026.2 jum

026.3 tokidoki

026.4 ALPHABETICAL ORDER

026.5 automatic art & design

026.1 Ariel Pintos

026.6 Carsten Raffel

026.7 ZIP Design

027.1 tokidoki

027.2 tokidoki

027.3 tokidoki

027.4 Jan Cafourek

027.5 Oscar Reyes

027.6 tokidoki

027.7 tokidoki

027.8 tokidoki

027.9 tokidoki

027.10 tokidoki

027.11 tokidoki

027.12 tokidoki

028.1 Dubius?

028.2 Rob Abeyta

028.3 WEWORKFORTHEM

028.4 Oscar Reyes

028.5 strange//attraktor

028.6 strange//attraktor

028.7 MK12 Design Studio

028.8 FLEAL

028.9 Formgeber

028.10 chemical box

028.11 lindedesign

028.12 lindedesign

029.1 MK12 Design Studio   029.2 MK12 Design Studio

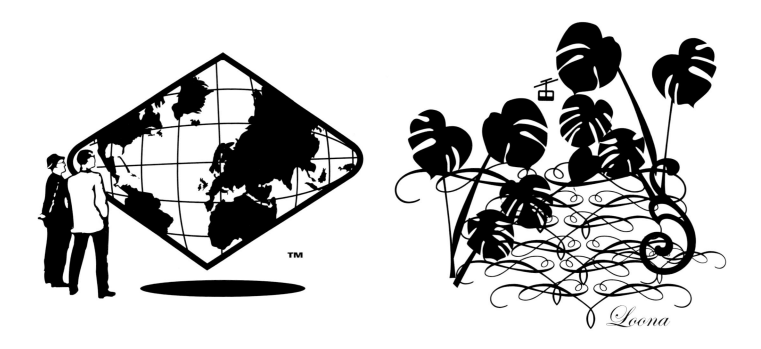

031.1 OCKTAK

031.2 PLEIX

032.1 strange//attraktor

032.2 nothing medialab

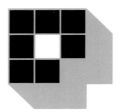

032.3 Formgeber

032.4 86 the onions

032.5 Theres Steiner

032.6 a+morph

032.7 FREITAG lab. ag

032.8 jum

032.9 Formgeber

033.1 no-domain

033.2 mikati

033.3 WEWORKFORTHEM

033.4 Gavillet & Rust

033.5 hirschindustries

033.6 Felix Braden

033.7 Jean-Jaques Tachdjian

033.8 Jürgen und ich

033.9 MK12 Design Studio

034.1 Jean-Jaques Tachdjian

034.2 bleed

034.3 bleed

034.4 bleed

034.5 FUTRO

034.6 FUTRO

035.1 Nendo Graphic Squad

035.2 Nendo Graphic Squad

035.3 Nendo Graphic Squad

035.4 Nendo Graphic Squad

036.1 Yuu Imokawa

036.2 Yuu Imokawa

036.3 bleed

036.4 stylodesign

036.5 KEEP LEFT STUDIO

036.6 stylodesign

036.7 WEWORKFORTHEM

036.8 METHOD

036.9 bleed

036.10 alphabetical order

036.11 dainippon type org.

036.12 bleed

037.1 stylodesign

037.2 Binnenland

037.3 WEWORKFORTHEM

037.4 KEEP LEFT STUDIO

037.5 VASAVA

037.6 WEWORKFORTHEM

038.1 FUTRO   038.2 Tina Backman   038.3 Formgeber   038.4 Felix Braden

038.5 Superlow   038.6 june   038.7 MetaDesign   038.8 Superlow

038.9 nothing medialab   038.10 FUTRO   038.11 Rinzen   038.12 METHOD

039.1 Hugh Morse Design

039.2 BLU DESIGN

039.3 BLU DESIGN

039.4 june

039.5 Nendo Graphic Squad

039.6 Hugh Morse Design

039.7 Jan Cafourek

039.8 MetaDesign

039.9 stylorouge

039.10 stylorouge

039.11 METHOD

039.12 Rikus Hilmann

040.1 ZIP Design

millésime
IN VINO VERITAS

040.2 Max Henschel

Jonathan Heyer
FOTOGRAFIE

040.3 Casarramona

040.4 tankdesign

040.5 Superlow

040.6 chemical box

Leutwyler Partner
Architekten

040.7 Theres Steiner

bührer
schön
wohnen

040.8 tankdesign

S C R E ≡ N
V ≡ S T

040.9 Um-bruch

roppongi hills - kanji characters   six trees   six circles as basic logo

六本木 ヒルズ゛ ＝  ＝ ○○○○ ○○

042.1 Max Henschel

042.2 june

042.3 KEEP LEFT STUDIO

042.4 KEEP LEFT STUDIO

042.5 POWER GRAPHIXX

042.6 Tsuyoshi Hirooka

042.7 moxi

042.8 chemical box

042.9 wuff design

043.1 june

043.2 june

043.3 june

043.4 bleed

043.5 bleed

043.6 VASAVA

043.7 Tsuyoshi Hirooka

043.8 Miguel Angel Leyva

043.9 viagrafik

044.1 inTEAM Graphics

044.2 viagrafik

044.3 bigsexyland

044.4 Masa Colectivo Gráfico

044.5 canefantasma studio

044.6 Raum Mannheim

044.7 KEEP LEFT STUDIO

044.8 stylodesign

044.9 J6Studios

044.10 J6Studios

044.11 strange//attraktor

044.12 chemical box

044.13 Ableton

044.14 Formgeber

044.15 Planet Pixel

044.16 Sebastian Gerbert

045.1 FORK UNSTABLE MEDIA

045.2 J6Studios

045.3 Dubius?

045.4 3Particles

045.5 ZIP Design

045.6 weissraum

045.7 weissraum

045.8 weissraum

045.9 weissraum

045.10 bleed

045.11 bleed

045.12 MetaDesign

045.13 MetaDesign

045.14 stylorouge

045.15 Kingsize

045.16 Nobody

046.1 Casarramona

046.2 Casarramona

046.3 Casarramona

046.4 Casarramona

047.1 Casarramona

047.2 Casarramona

047.3 Balsi Grafik

047.4 rosendahlgrafik

047.5 stylorouge

047.6 zookeeper

047.7 J6Studios

047.8 HandGun

047.9 weissraum

047.10 Kingsize

047.11 Hula Hula

047.12 Gianni Rossi

047.13 weissraum

047.14 weissraum

047.15 MK12 Design Studio

047.16 shida keiichi design

DRAGON SOUR
style store event

PÆRESMAK
梨の実

048.1 weissraum   048.2 bleed

049.1 KEEP LEFT STUDIO

049.2 strange//attraktor

049.3 bionic-systems

049.4 Tsuyoshi Hirooka

050.1 bionic-systems

050.2 Felix Braden

050.3 jum

050.4 Masa Colectivo Gráfico

051.1 MK12 Design Studio

051.2 Hausgrafik

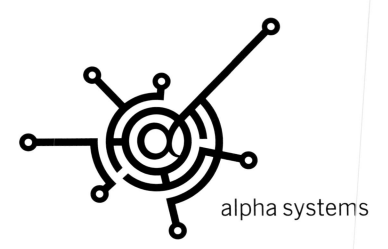

051.3 Axel Raidt

051.4 shida keiichi design

052.1 Chris Hutchinson

052.2 weissraum

052.3 stylodesign

052.4 Ableton

052.5 stylodesign

052.6 MK12 Design Studio

052.7 VASAVA

052.8 plumnotion

052.9 stylorouge

052.10 strange//attraktor

052.11 plumnotion

052.12 DESIGNGARTEN

053.1 B.ü.L.b grafix

053.2 ala webstatt

053.3 Hula Hula

053.4 weissraum

053.5 lindedesign

053.6 plumnotion

053.7 Gianni Rossi

053.8 Gianni Rossi

053.9 the brainbox

053.10 Casarramona

054.1 tokidoki

054.2 MK12 Design Studio

054.3 Kallegraphics

054.4 zookeeper

054.5 tokidoki

054.6 tokidoki

055.1 Hula Hula

055.2 ZIP Design

055.3 weissraum

055.4 weissraum

055.5 KEEP LEFT STUDIO

055.6 moxi

055.7 316tn

055.8 Nobody

055.9 jum

055.10 Max Henschel

055.11 weissraum

055.12 Kallegraphics

056.1 superfamous

056.2 J6Studios

056.3 VASAVA

056.4 MK12 Design Studio

056.5 VASAVA

056.6 52NORD

056.7 ZIP Design

056.8 KEEP LEFT STUDIO

056.9 hirschindustries

056.10 Io Design

056.11 automatic art & design

056.12 Hula Hula

CAMDENS

057.1 METHOD

simmental
suisse

057.2 Kong

groovesound

057.3 Kong

StudioDirect

057.4 METHOD

Novamedia
NEW MEDIA AGENCY

057.5 canefantasma studio

Greville Ingham group

057.6 KEEP LEFT STUDIO

dotbank

057.7 METHOD

THE OCTONAUTS

057.8 Meomi Design

BUMPERSTUDIO
バンパースタジオ

057.9 VASAVA

Firma
Aqua Coastal and
Estuarine Consulting

057.10 KEEP LEFT STUDIO

institut für
raumfreiheit
MÖBEL·OBJEKTE·INNENEINRICHTUNG

057.11 Formgeber

STREIFENEDER
TRADING
INDUSTRIES

057.12 Um-bruch

058.1 Um-bruch

058.2 Um-bruch

058.3 WG Berlin

058.4 WG Berlin

058.5 Yuu Imokawa

058.6 Gabor Palotai

058.7 bionic-systems

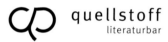

058.8 NULLPROZENTFETT

058.9 VASAVA

058.10 Niels Jansson

058.11 jum

058.12 hirschindustries

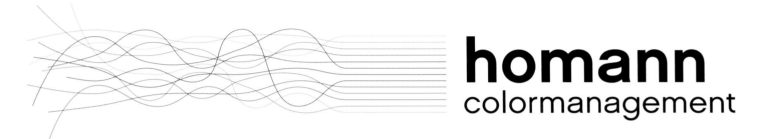

059.1 rosendahlgrafik

059.2 Masa Colectivo Gráfico   059.3 MK12 Design Studio   059.4 BlackJune   059.5 Masa Colectivo Gráfico

059.6 Masa Colectivo Gráfico   059.7 weissraum   059.8 PFADFINDEREI   059.9 weissraum

060.1 Tsuyoshi Kusano

060.2 viagrafik

060.3 Chris Hutchinson

060.4 strange//attraktor

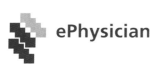

060.5 METHOD

060.6 METHOD

060.7 Nendo Graphic Squad

060.8 typotherapy

060.9 nothing medialab

060.10 nothing medialab

060.11 Planet Pixel

060.12 nothing medialab

060.13 Nobody

060.14 Nobody

060.15 METHOD

060.16 Formgeber

061.1 minigram

061.2 Zion Graphics

061.3 OCKTAK

061.4 Unit Delta Plus

061.5 J6Studios

061.6 Pia Kolle

061.7 Nobody

061.8 Nobody

061.9 chemical box

061.10 METHOD

061.11 viagrafik

061.12 moxi

061.13 Hula Hula

061.14 Max Henschel

061.15 BlackJune

061.16 Nendo Graphic Squad

062.1 Binnenland

062.2 BlackJune

062.3 stylodesign

062.4 stylodesign

062.5 typotherapy

062.6 shida keiichi design

STEFAN VORLOB [R]

062.7 minigram

062.8 cubegrafik

062.9 weissraum

LETZISTRASSE 23 8006 CH–ZÜRICH HERZOGGEISSLER

063.1 Theres Steiner

063.2 cubegrafik

063.3 Masa Colectivo Gráfico

063.4 Tsuyoshi Hirooka

063.5 Dubius?

063.6 cubegrafik

063.7 cubegrafik

063.8 strange//attraktor

063.9 GWG CO. LTD

063.10 BlackJune

063.11 FORK UNSTABLE MEDIA

063.12 BlackJune

063.13 zookeeper

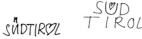

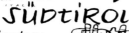

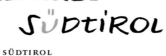
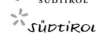

064.1 MetaDesign

064.2 nu designs+ yanku

064.3 nu designs+ yanku

065.1 Markus Moström Design

065.2 Markus Moström Design

065.3 Markus Moström Design

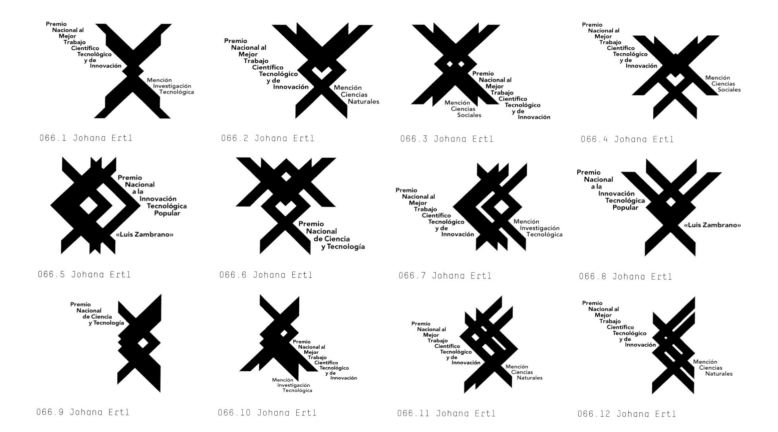

066.1 Johana Ertl

066.2 Johana Ertl

066.3 Johana Ertl

066.4 Johana Ertl

066.5 Johana Ertl

066.6 Johana Ertl

066.7 Johana Ertl

066.8 Johana Ertl

066.9 Johana Ertl

066.10 Johana Ertl

066.11 Johana Ertl

066.12 Johana Ertl

067.1 dainippon type org.   067.2 Tsuyoshi Hirooka   067.3 Maniackers Design   067.4 Maniackers Design

067.5 NULLPROZENTFETT   067.6 Nobody

067.7 Nendo Graphic Squad   067.8 Masa Colectivo Gráfico

CULTURE

KULTUR

Museums and openings, galleries and exhibitions, stage and stalls, fine artists and performers – a richly varied subject making heavy demands on design. This chapter shows current examples of exciting new work in a whole range of cultural fields.

Museen und Vernissagen, Galerien und Ausstellungen, Bühne und Parkett, bildende Künstler und Performer – ein façettenreiches Thema, das hohe Designansprüche stellt. Dieses Kapitel zeigt aktuelle Beispiele, wie auf den unterschiedlichsten Gebieten der Kultur Zeichen gesetzt werden.

HAPPYPETS PRODUCTS

"A LOGO MAY NOT BE TOTALLY ACCESSIBLE ON A FIRST READING."

Where do you get inspiration for your work?
The inspiration for our work comes from the contrasts that go to make our daily lives now. We feel attracted by everything that seems paradoxical in some way – two environments and constellations that are complete opposites and that we include in our work. For example nature/technology, naïve/monstrous, violence/absurdity, construction/sketch, sex/consumption.

Do you work according to a definite design philosophy?
Our design philosophy could be Happypets/Happypeople. We like to see our work as a bit absurd, off the wall. We want our work to be fun, we want to create, test, do; it's a kind of design craving. We live out a philosophy of movement, of doing and not of stagnation. Nevertheless the most important idea is of course always to communicate something, a mood, a message – and in this context the content is always more important than the form.

What would you say is the key to a good, successful logo?
We think a great logo is one that tells a story, conveys an atmosphere, a context; it is not necessarily simple or pure and reduced. Generally a logo is more than the idea of presenting something complex simply. Our approach suggests that a logo can be very complicated and loud. It has to make a big visual impact, but we like to be able to come back to it from time to time to analyse it. And we also like it if it is not totally accessible on a first reading.

Do your aesthetic values and your clients' demands ever clash?
Fundamentally we try to work only with people who understand that out aesthetic values are very important to us and have to be developed further.

If a client wasn't prepared to accept your work, how far would you be prepared to compromise?
We always set up a dialogue with our clients before we start a project so that they understand our approach. Even so: if our creative input doesn't suit what they want – for example because of opposing aesthetic approaches, then the client doesn't need our solution. We have realised that in general compromises are solutions that do not satisfy anyone … and that make us lose sleep. Put another way: a compromise is not a solution, but a dialogue is always a good idea.

Happypets Products, Lausanne, Switzerland | www.happypets.ch

Wo holt ihr euch die Inspirationen für eure Arbeit?
Die Inspiration für unsere Arbeit kommt von den Kontrasten, die das Alltagsleben heutzutage prägen. Wir fühlen uns von allem angezogen, was irgendwie paradox erscheint – zwei Umgebungen und Konstellationen, die total gegensätzlich sind und die wir in unsere Arbeit einbeziehen. Zum Beispiel Natur/Technologie, naiv/monströs, Gewalt/Absurdität, Konstruktion/Sketch, Sex/Konsum.

Arbeitet ihr nach einer definierten Designphilosophie?
Unsere Designphilosophie könnte lauten: Happypets/Happypeople. Wir lieben es, unsere Arbeit als ein wenig absurd, als abgehoben zu bezeichnen. Wir wollen, dass uns unsere Arbeit Spass macht, wir wollen kreieren, testen, machen; es ist so eine Art Design-Heisshunger. Wie leben eine Philosophie der Bewegung, des Machens und nicht der Stagnation. Trotzdem ist die wichtigste Idee natürlich immer, etwas zu kommunizieren, eine Stimmung, eine Message – und in diesem Kontext ist der Inhalt stets wichtiger als die Form.

Was charakterisiert in euren Augen ein gutes, ein gelungenes Logo?
Unserer Meinung nach ist ein grosses Logo eines, das eine Geschichte erzählt, eine Atmosphäre transportiert, ein Umfeld; es ist nicht unbedingt einfach oder pur und reduziert. Generell ist ein Logo mehr als die Idee, etwas Komplexes einfach darzustellen. Nach unserer Denkweise kann ein Logo sehr kompliziert und laut sein. Sein visueller Impact muss stark sein, aber wir lieben es, von Zeit zu Zeit darauf zurück kommen zu können, um es zu analysieren. Und wir mögen es auch, wenn es sich bei der ersten Betrachtung nicht gleich völlig erschließt.

Gibt's Konflikte zwischen euren ästhetischen Wertvorstellungen und den Ansprüchen eurer Kunden?
Grundsätzlich versuchen wir nur mit Leuten zu arbeiten, die verstehen, dass uns unsere ästhetischen Wertvorstellungen sehr wichtig sind und weiterentwickelt werden müssen.

Angenommen, ein Kunde akzeptiert eure Arbeit nicht: Wie weit lasst ihr euch dann auf Kompromisse ein?
Damit der Kunde unsere Auffassung versteht, initiieren wir jeweils einen Dialog, bevor wir mit einem Projekt beginnen. Trotzdem: Wenn unser kreativer Input für seine Lösung nicht akzeptiert wird – zum Beispiel wegen konträrer ästhetischer Auffassungen, dann braucht der Kunde unsere Lösung nicht. Generell haben wir realisiert, dass Kompromisse Lösungen sind, die keinen befriedigen… und uns den Schlaf rauben. Anders gesagt: Ein Kompromiss ist keine Lösung, aber ein Dialog ist immer eine gute Idee.

Happypets Products, Lausanne, Schweiz | www.happypets.ch

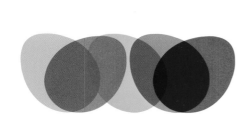

070.1 INSECT

070.2 MetaDesign

070.3 FUTRO

070.4 MARTIN WOODTLI

070.5 MARTIN WOODTLI

070.6 MARTIN WOODTLI

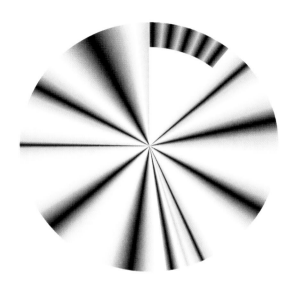

071.1 Surface

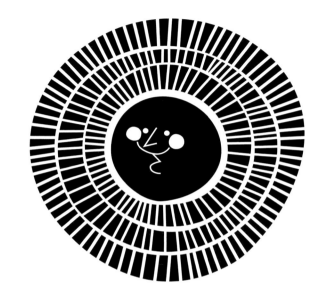

071.2 FLEAL

071.3 Syrup Helsinki   071.4 FLEAL   071.5 Tsuyoshi Kusano   071.6 Jürgen und ich

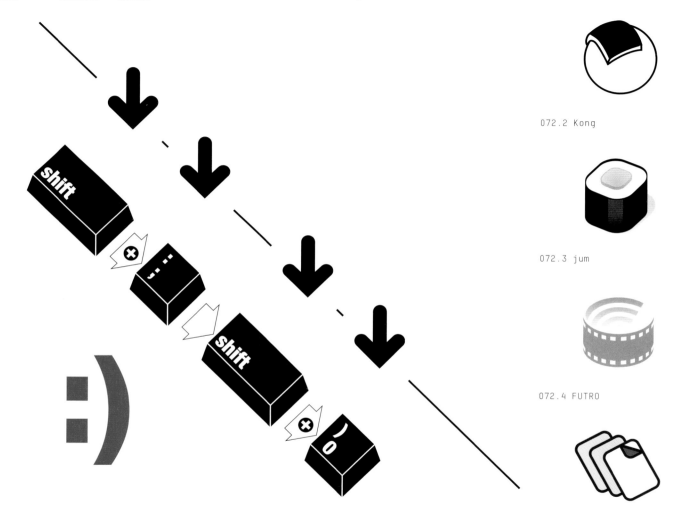

072.2 Kong

072.3 jum

072.4 FUTRO

072.1 FLEAL

072.5 TAK!

073.1 Carsten Raffel

073.2 Carsten Raffel

073.3 jum

073.4 tokidoki

073.5 Happypets Products

073.6 Happypets Products

073.7 Happypets Products

073.8 Happypets Products

073.9 Happypets Products

073.10 Happypets Products

073.11 Happypets Products

073.12 Happypets Products

073.13 Happypets Products

073.14 Happypets Products

073.15 Happypets Products

073.16 Happypets Products

074.1 Thorsten Geiger

074.2 Happypets Products

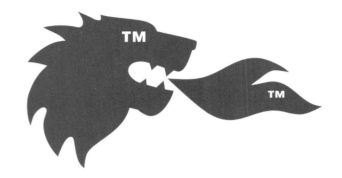

074.3 Happypets Products

074.4 Felix Braden

074.5 Syrup Helsinki

074.6 stylodesign

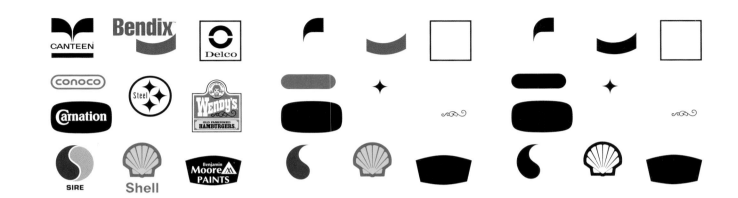

075.1 Happypets Products

075.2 Happypets Products

076.1 Happypets Products

076.2 Happypets Products

076.3 Happypets Products

076.4 Happypets Products

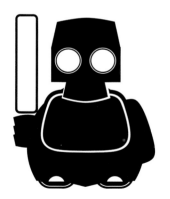

076.5 Happypets Products

076.6 Happypets Products

076.7 Happypets Products

076.8 Happypets Products

077.1 Happypets Products

077.2 Happypets Products

077.3 Happypets Products

077.4 Happypets Products

077.5 Happypets Products

077.6 Happypets Products

077.7 Happypets Products

077.8 Happypets Products

077.9 Happypets Products

077.10 Happypets Products

077.11 Happypets Products

077.12 Happypets Products

077.13 Happypets Products

077.14 Happypets Products

077.15 Happypets Products

077.16 Happypets Products

078.1 Happypets Products

078.2 Happypets Products

078.3 Happypets Products

078.4 Happypets Products

078.5 Happypets Products

078.6 Happypets Products

079.1 Happypets Products

079.2 Happypets Products

079.3 Happypets Products

079.4 Happypets Products

079.5 Happypets Products

079.6 Happypets Products

080.1 MK12 Design Studio

080.2 MK12 Design Studio   080.3 Norm   080.4 MK12 Design Studio

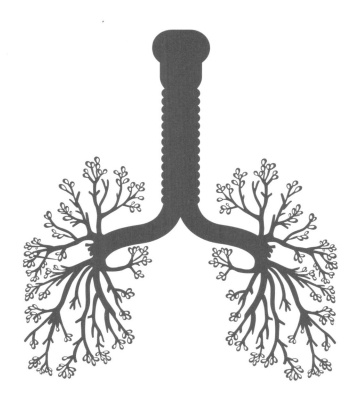

081.1 MK12 Design Studio

081.2 MK12 Design Studio

082.1 Nendo Graphic Squad

082.2 Nendo Graphic Squad

083.1 Digitalultras

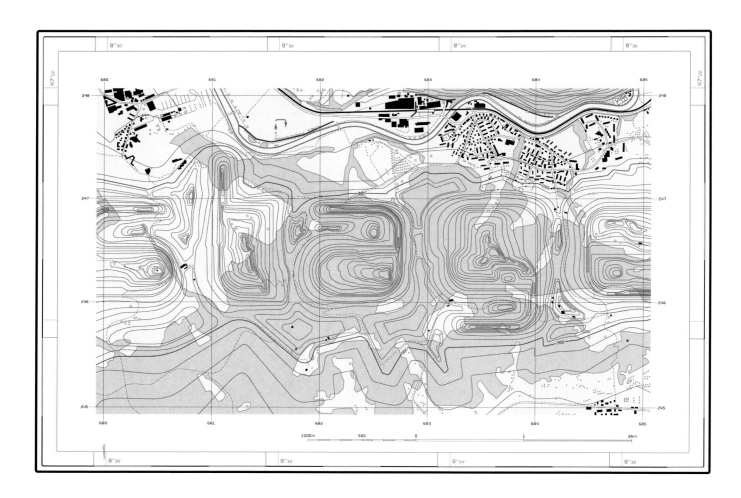

084.1 MARTIN WOODTLI

085.1 MARTIN WOODTLI

085.2 MARTIN WOODTLI

085.3 MARTIN WOODTLI

085.4 MARTIN WOODTLI

085.5 MARTIN WOODTLI

085.6 Maniackers Design

085.7 struggle inc

086.1 Norm

086.2 Norm

086.3 Norm

086.4 Norm

086.5 Karen Ingram

086.6 A-Side Studio

086.7 KEEP LEFT STUDIO

086.8 Kong

087.1 viagrafik

087.2 nu designs+ yanku

087.3 Gavillet & Rust

087.4 bleed

087.5 Rinzen

087.6 Niels Jansson

087.7 Nendo Graphic Squad

087.8 Nendo Graphic Squad

087.9 Nendo Graphic Squad

panorama

088.1 blindresearch

HYDROPHOBIA SERIES
ANNO DOMINI MMIII

088.2 Superlow

ヮﾏﾑﾑ ﾛﾛﾚﾛ®

088.3 bionic-systems

black pearl

088.4 Max Henschel

URBANSKILS

088.5 BÜRO DESTRUCT

088.6 Lisa Schibel

diffusion   de La Tour   shorts!

089.1 studiotonne   089.2 moxi   089.3 310 K

the farm   nation™

089.4 Rinzen   089.5 viagrafik   089.6 KEEP LEFT STUDIO

M°ARS   TIRAN[i]A   pharo™

089.7 FUTRO   089.8 VASAVA   089.9 KEEP LEFT STUDIO

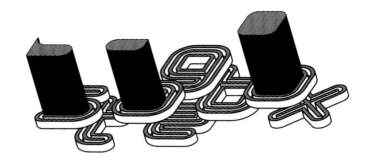

090.1 VASAVA

090.2 MARTIN WOODTLI

090.3 HandGun

090.4 viagrafik

091.1 MetaDesign

091.2 doublestandards

091.3 doublestandards

091.4 Dubius?

091.5 POWER GRAPHIXX

091.6 Rinzen

091.7 Norm

091.8 B.ü.L.b grafix

091.9 Gabor Palotai

092.1 jutojo

092.2 jutojo

092.3 Factor Produkt

092.4 A´

092.5 A´

092.6 bleed

092.7 strange//attraktor

092.8 Jean-Jaques Tachdjian

092.9 FROZT

093.1 moxi

093.2 HandGun

093.3 Gianni Rossi

093.4 Ariel Pintos

093.5 3Particles

093.6 nothing medialab

093.7 zookeeper

093.8 Jean-Jaques Tachdjian

093.9 Ophorus

094.1 FLEAL

094.2 FLEAL

094.3 FLEAL

094.4 Ariel Pintos

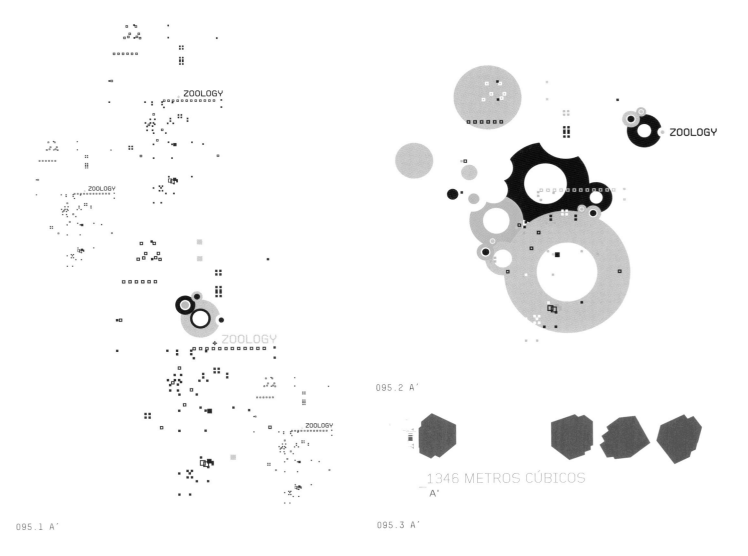

ZOOLOGY

ZOOLOGY

ZOOLOGY

ZOOLOGY

ZOOLOGY

1346 METROS CÚBICOS

A'

095.2 A'

095.1 A'

095.3 A'

096.1 Factor Produkt

096.2 struggle inc

096.3 Max Henschel

096.4 doublestandards

096.5 doublestandards

096.6 doublestandards

William Shakespeare **Hamlet**

THE SKY

AIM FOR THE SKY

098.1 doublestandards

098.2 doublestandards

098.3 doublestandards

098.4 Sanjai

098.5 Sanjai

098.6 Sanjai

098.7 Sanjai

098.8 Sanjai

098.9 Sanjai

099.1 Superlow

099.2 Kong

099.3 viagrafik

099.4 INSECT

099.5 A-Side Studio

099.6 a+morph

099.7 a+morph

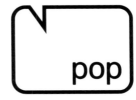

099.8 doublestandards

099.9 jutojo

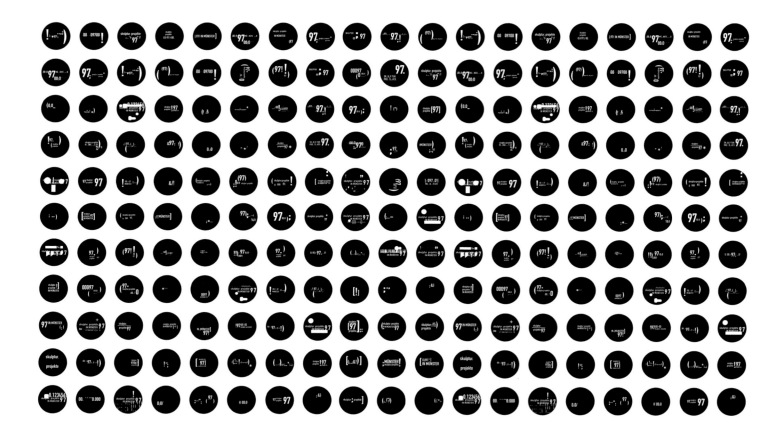

100.1 doublestandards

101.1 Positron

101.2 doublestandards

102.1 tankdesign

102.2 a small percent

102.3 Masa Colectivo Gráfico

102.4 A´

103.1 plumnotion

103.2 zorglob

103.3 Lisa Schibel

103.4 Um-bruch

103.5 mikati

103.6 METHOD

103.7 viagrafik

103.8 Axel Raidt

103.9 doublestandards

104.1 Max Henschel

104.2 mission design agency

EUROPANZON

104.3 Superlow

104.4 FUTRO

scrollen

104.5 Io Design

ICONOGRAPHIC

104.6 stylodesign

105.1 Carine Abraham

105.2 struggle inc

105.3 viagrafik

105.4 viagrafik

105.5 BlackJune

105.6 Nonstop

105.7 Felix Braden

105.8 the brainbox

105.9 Furi Furi

106.1 the brainbox

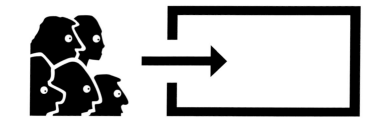

106.2 310 K

106.3 Lisa Schibel

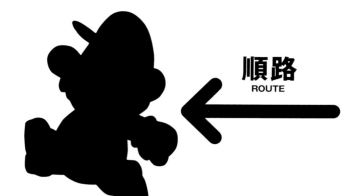

106.4 Tsuyoshi Kusano

107.1 KEEP LEFT STUDIO

107.2 the brainbox

107.3 KEEP LEFT STUDIO

107.4 Happypets Products

108.1 fulguro

108.2 fulguro

108.3 fulguro

109.1 fulguro

109.2 fulguro

110.1 Barnbrook Design

110.2 Barnbrook Design

110.3 Barnbrook Design

110.4 Barnbrook Design

110.5 Barnbrook Design

110.6 Barnbrook Design

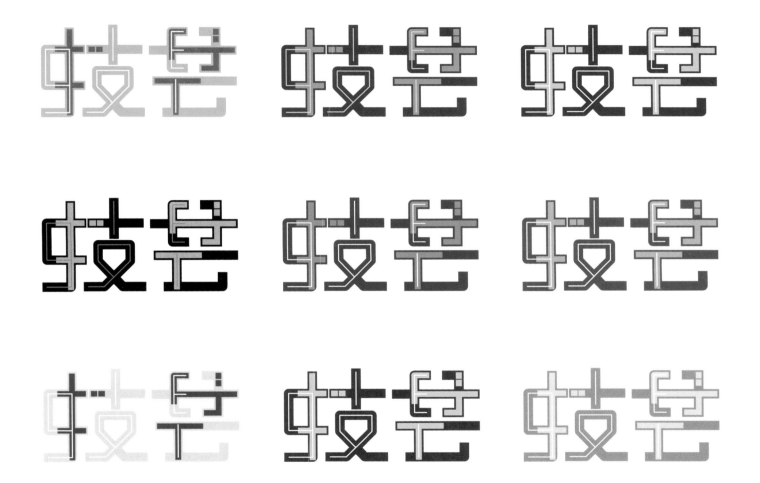

111.1 dainippon type org.

DESIGN

DESIGN

How do designers handle self-images reduced to signs? An exciting question, answered in 1001 different ways in this chapter.

Wie halten es Gestalter mit ihren auf Zeichen reduzierten Selbstdarstellungen? Eine spannende Frage, die in diesem Kapitel auf 1001 verschiedene Arten beantwortet wird.

„EIN LOGO DARF AUCH SEHGEWOHNHEITEN BRECHEN."

Where do you get inspiration for your work?
We get inspiration for our work from a whole range of things. A short survey: WIM CROUWEL, H.P. WILLBERG, SQUAREPUSHER, CONVERGE, J. MÜLLER-BROCKMANN, DADA & RAOUL HAUSMANN, SITUATIONISTS, NIETZSCHE, SARTRE, HENRY MILLER, ANAÏS NIN, GEORG BÜCHNER, REFUSED, ORCHID, SCIENCE-FICTION, CHAOS / ORDER, LOVE / HATE, VARIETY OF HUMANS, DELTA, KARL MARX, Z. HADID, GILLIAMS BRAZIL, MK12, BÜRO DESTRUCT, LUCA IONESCU, MONTY PYTHON, ALIEN, BLADE RUNNER, GHOST IN THE SHELL, PI, BUILD, DEJOE, KHC ...

Do you work according to a definite design philosophy?
From wall to screen to everything, we've only got our boredom to lose ...

What would you say is the key to a good, successful logo?
A good logo is in one or two colours, it reproduces well in all media and is highly recognisable. But a logo can also change our usual way of looking at things and question old values, it has to have enough character to be able to remain timeless. A good logo is "catchy", it should be pleasing to the eye.

Do your aesthetic values and your clients' demands ever clash?
Yes, but we try to realise as many projects as possible where the client trusts us.

If a client wasn't prepared to accept your work, how far would you be prepared to compromise?
Unfortunately the customer is still king. You can try to talk them into the better variant, but if their partner thinks round shapes are "nicer" and you design is based on a square you'll have to go back to the drawing-board. But usually a logo is convincing at first glance and major corrections aren't needed.

Viagrafik, Wiesbaden, Germany | www.viagrafik.com

Wo holt ihr euch die Inspirationen für eure Arbeit?
Inspiration für unsere Arbeit finden wir in ganz unterschiedlichen Dingen. Ein kleiner Überblick: WIM CROUWEL, H.P. WILLBERG, SQUAREPUSHER, CONVERGE, J. MÜLLER-BROCKMANN, DADA & RAOUL HAUSMANN, SITUATIONISTEN, NIETZSCHE, SARTRE, HENRY MILLER, ANAÏS NIN, GEORG BÜCHNER, REFUSED, ORCHID, SCIENCE-FICTION, CHAOS / ORDER, LOVE / HATE, VARIETY OF HUMANS, DELTA, KARL MARX, Z. HADID, GILLIAMS BRAZIL, MK12, BÜRO DESTRUCT, LUCA IONESCU, MONTY PYTHON, ALIEN, BLADE RUNNER, GHOST IN THE SHELL, PI, BUILD, DEJOE, KHC,...

Arbeitet ihr nach einer definierten Designphilosophie?
From wall to screen to everything, we only got our boredom to lose...

Was charakterisiert in euren Augen ein gutes, ein gelungenes Logo?
Ein gutes Logo ist ein – oder zweifarbig, es ist in allen Medien gut reproduzierbar und weist ein hohes Maß an Wiedererkennungswert auf. Ein Logo darf aber auch Sehgewohnheiten brechen und Altes in Frage stellen, es muss genügend Charakter besitzen, um zeitlos bleiben zu können. Ein gutes Logo ist „catchy", das Auge soll sich an ihm erfreuen.

Gibt's Konflikte zwischen euren ästhetischen Wertvorstellungen und den Ansprüchen eurer Kunden?
Ja, aber wir versuchen möglichst viele Projekte zu realisieren, wo der Kunde uns vertraut.

Angenommen, ein Kunde akzeptiert eure Arbeit nicht: Wie weit lasst ihr euch dann auf Kompromisse ein?
Leider bleibt der Kunde König. Man kann zwar versuchen, ihn von der besseren Variante zu überzeugen, doch wenn der Lebensgefährte runde Formen „schöner" findet und dein Entwurf auf einem Quadrat basiert, wirst du noch mal neu anfangen müssen. Normalerweise überzeugt aber ein Logo auf den ersten Blick, und eine grössere Korrektur bleibt aus.

Viagrafik, Wiesbaden, Deutschland | www.viagrafik.com

•

114.1 Tsuyoshi Hirooka

114.2 Formgeber

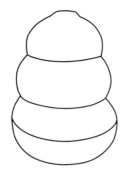

114.3 Kong

114.4 NULLPROZENTFETT

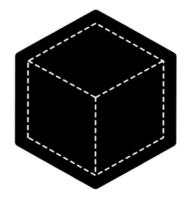

114.5 Formgeber

114.6 Felix Braden

115.1 Peter Vattanatham

115.2 dopepope

115.3 OCKTAK

115.4 Maniackers Design

115.5 Maniackers Design

115.6 strange//attraktor

115.7 plumnotion

115.8 dopepope

115.9 Sebastian Gerbert

115.10 Sebastian Gerbert

115.11 Sebastian Gerbert

115.12 Sebastian Gerbert

116.1 OSCREY

117.1 fulguro

118.1 fulguro

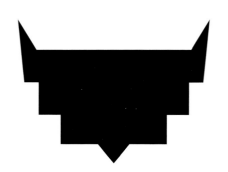

118.2 fulguro

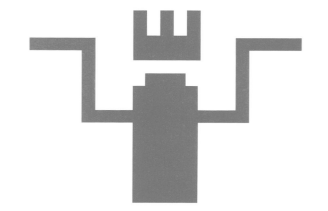

118.3 WG Berlin

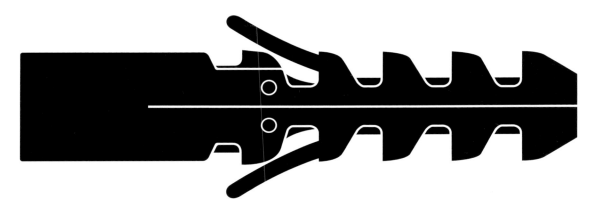

119.1 viagrafik

119.2 Tsuyoshi Kusano   119.3 Nonstop   119.4 BÜRO DESTRUCT

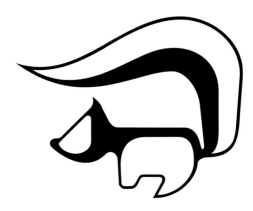

120.1 BORDFUNK

120.2 Gianni Rossi

120.3 Gianni Rossi

120.6 Gianni Rossi

120.7 Gianni Rossi

120.4 Gozer Media

120.5 INSECT

120.8 FUTRO

120.9 Nendo Graphic Squad

121.1 Kallegraphics

121.2 Zion Graphics

121.3 Rebel One

121.4 OSCREY

121.5 plumnotion

121.6 tokidoki

122.1 OSCREY

122.2 no-domain

122.3 FLEAL

122.4 WG Berlin

123.1 ohiogirl Design   123.2 ohiogirl Design

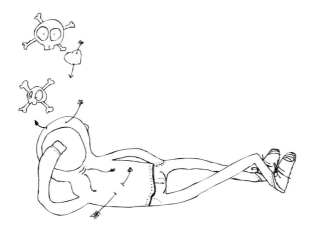

124.1 fupete studio

124.2 fupete studio

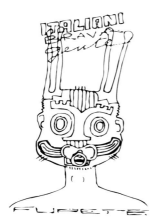

124.3 fupete studio

124.4 fupete studio

124.5 fupete studio

125.1 FLEAL

126.1 Formgeber

126.2 viagrafik

126.3 weissraum

126.4 tokidoki

126.5 tokidoki

126.6 tokidoki

126.7 tokidoki

126.8 Oscar Salinas Losada

126.9 Studio Süd

126.10 tokidoki

126.11 tokidoki

126.12 tokidoki

127.1 Rebel One

127.2 Rebel One

127.3 Rebel One

127.4 Rebel One

127.5 ZIP Design

127.6 Hausgrafik

128.1 Gianni Rossi

128.2 NULLPROZENTFETT

128.3 Oscar Salinas Losada

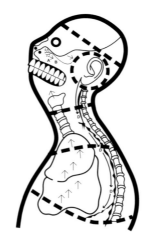

128.4 FLEAL

128.5 Masa Colectivo Gráfico

129.1 Syrup Helsinki

129.2 Gianni Rossi

129.3 dopepope

129.4 Jürgen und ich

129.5 dopepope

129.6 dopepope

129.7 dopepope

130.1 Happypets Products

130.2 Happypets Products

130.3 Happypets Products

130.4 Happypets Products

130.5 Happypets Products

130.6 Happypets Products

131.1 Happypets Products

131.2 Happypets Products

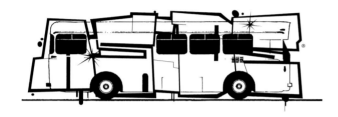

132.1 A-Side Studio

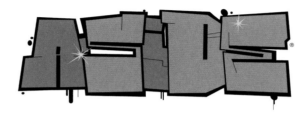

132.2 A-Side Studio

132.3 A-Side Studio

132.4 A-Side Studio

132.5 jum

132.6 viagrafik

133.1 Ariel Pintos

133.2 Gabor Palotai

133.3 Hort

133.4 ohiogirl Design

133.5 fulguro

133.6 FROZT

133.7 everyday icons

133.8 polygraph

133.9 Raum Mannheim

133.10 alphabetical order

133.11 KEEP LEFT STUDIO

133.12 sweaterweather

134.1 Hort

134.2 Hort

134.3 Hort

134.4 sweaterweather

134.5 superfamous

134.6 Maniackers Design

134.7 Gabor Palotai

Vik

134.8 sweaterweather

134.9 Maniackers Design

134.10 GWG CO. LTD

134.11 Karen Ingram

134.12 sweaterweather

134.13 Carsten Raffel

134.14 Vår

134.15 superfamous

134.16 sweaterweather

135.1 Belmer Negrillo

135.2 a small percent

135.3 a+morph

135.4 viagrafik

135.5 polygraph

135.6 viagrafik

135.7 polygraph

135.8 sunrise studios

135.9 Maniackers Design

135.10 Maniackers Design

135.11 mikati

135.12 Ariel Pintos

135.13 MAGNETOFONICAOFONICA

135.14 viagrafik

135.15 viagrafik

135.16 Jean-Jaques Tachdjian

136.1 viagrafik

136.2 viagrafik

136.3 viagrafik

136.4 viagrafik

136.5 viagrafik

136.6 viagrafik

136.7 viagrafik

136.8 viagrafik

136.9 viagrafik

136.10 viagrafik

136.11 viagrafik

136.12 viagrafik

137.1 Hort

137.2 Hort

137.3 Hort

137.4 Hort

137.5 Hort

137.6 Hort

137.7 Hort

137.8 Hort

137.9 Hort

137.10 Hort

137.11 ohiogirl Design

137.12 ohiogirl Design

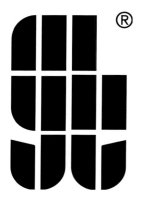

138.1 viagrafik

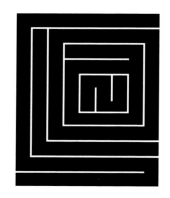

138.2 Mark Sloan

138.3 polygraph

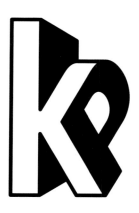

138.4 polygraph

138.5 Carsten Raffel

138.6 Io Design

139.1 dopepope

139.2 dopepope

139.3 dopepope

139.4 dopepope

139.5 dopepope

139.6 dopepope

139.7 Dubius?

139.8 Dubius?

139.9 Dubius?

140.1 Kallegraphics

viagrafik

140.2 viagrafik

140.3 Furi Furi

140.4 viagrafik

140.5 weissraum

nudesigns+

140.6 nu designs+ yanku

141.1 no-domain

141.2 mikati

saturate™

141.3 superfamous

141.4 Oscar Salinas Losada

141.5 Hula Hula

141.6 Oscar Salinas Losada

142.1 MAGNETOFONICA

142.2 BÜRO DESTRUCT

142.3 NULLPROZENTFETT

142.4 bleed

142.5 Mark Sloan

142.6 viagrafik

143.1 fupete studio

143.2 bionic-systems

143.3 HandGun

143.4 Felix Braden

—

144.1 eboy

144.2 eboy

144.3 eboy

144.4 eboy

144.5 eboy

144.6 A-Side Studio

145.1 KEEP LEFT STUDIO

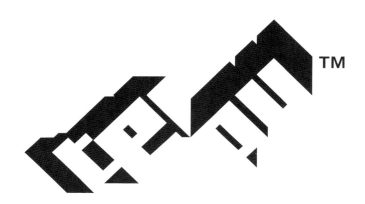

146.1 bleed

146.2 A-Side Studio

146.3 HandGun

146.4 dmote

147.1 ZIP Design

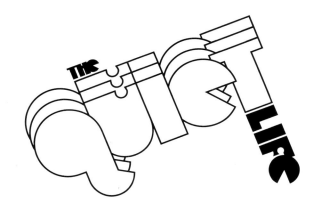

147.2 ohiogirl Design

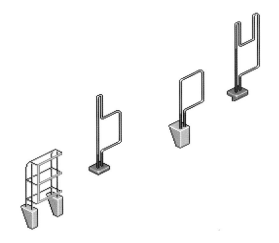

147.3 eboy

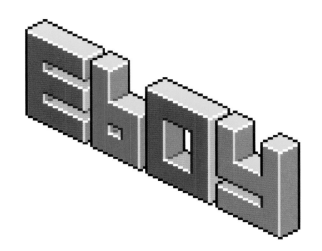

147.4 eboy

148.1 INSECT

148.2 ZIP Design

148.3 strange//attraktor

148.4 KEEP LEFT STUDIO

149.1 Oscar Salinas Losada

149.2 ZIP Design

149.3 ZIP Design

149.4 Masa Colectivo Gráfico

150.1 Rebel One

150.2 ZIP Design

150.3 zookeeper

150.4 zookeeper

Against Wrong™

151.1 Unit Delta Plus

151.2 Raum Mannheim

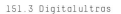

151.3 Digitalultras

151.4 Digitalultras

151.5 POWER GRAPHIXX

151.6 KEEP LEFT STUDIO

152.1 J6Studios

152.2 NULLPROZENTFETT

152.3 A´

152.4 BÜRO DESTRUCT

152.5 Max Henschel

152.6 blindresearch

153.1 no-domain

153.2 Rebel One

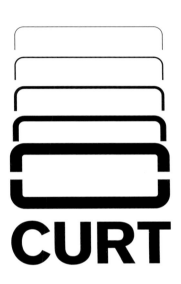

153.3 Sebastian Gerbert

153.4 Chris Hutchinson

153.5 fulguro

153.6 fupete studio

154.1 canefantasma studio

154.2 jum

154.3 viagrafik

154.4 Rebel One

154.5 dopepope

154.6 Nonstop

154.7 symbolodesign

154.8 struggle inc

154.9 A-Side Studio

155.1 Maniackers Design

155.2 Maniackers Design

155.3 weissraum

155.4 Carsten Raffel

155.5 inkgraphix

155.6 REGINA

155.7 Meomi Design

155.8 Maniackers Design

155.9 viagrafik

156.1 bleed

156.2 Formgeber

156.3 zorglob

156.4 blindresearch

156.5 J6Studios

156.6 bleed

156.7 everyday icons

156.8 jum

156.9 inkgraphix

157.1 ohiogirl Design

157.2 ohiogirl Design

157.3 ohiogirl Design

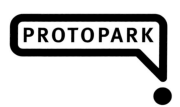

158.1 Alexander Fuchs

158.2 viagrafik

158.3 MAGNETOFONICA

158.4 ohiogirl Design

158.5 ohiogirl Design

158.6 ohiogirl Design

158.7 WG Berlin

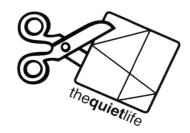

158.8 Studio Süd

158.9 Masa Colectivo Gráfico

159.1 New Future People

159.2 COLOURMOVIE

159.3 Dokhaus

159.4 Felix Braden

159.5 dopepope

159.6 GWG CO. LTD

159.7 J6Studios

159.8 Hula Hula

159.9 Jürgen und ich

159.10 stylodesign

159.11 zookeeper

159.12 ohiogirl Design

159.13 J6Studios

159.14 Masa Colectivo Gráfico

159.15 Rebel One

159.16 Planet Pixel

160.1 wuff design

160.2 symbolodesign

160.3 bionic-systems

161.1 zookeeper

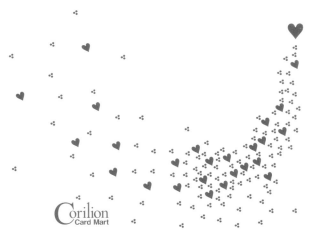

161.2 New Future People

161.3 Syrup Helsinki

162.1 weissraum

162.2 BLU DESIGN

162.3 Hula Hula

162.4 Hula Hula

162.5 Felix Braden

162.6 canefantasma studio

162.7 Propella

162.8 Felix Braden

162.9 tokidoki

162.10 tokidoki

162.11 REGINA

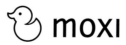

162.12 moxi

163.1 tokidoki

163.2 pee & poo

164.1 Max Henschel

164.2 Max Henschel

164.3 INSECT

164.4 zorglob

164.5 BÜRO DESTRUCT

164.6 GWG CO. LTD

164.7 sunrise studios

164.8 Karlssonwilker Inc.

164.9 86 the onions

164.10 FORK UNSTABLE MEDIA

164.11 HandGun

164.12 Hula Hula

165.1 Superlow

165.2 viagrafik

165.3 sunrise studios

165.4 urbn;

165.5 viagrafik

165.6 Gianni Rossi

166.1 A´

166.2 A´

166.3 A´

166.4 A´

166.5 weissraum

166.6 BlackJune

166.7 polygraph

166.8 Dokhaus

166.9 dopepope

166.10 PFADFINDEREI

166.11 viagrafik

166.12 HandGun

167.1 cubegrafik

167.2 Maniackers Design

167.3 Nendo Graphic Squad

167.4 Syrup Helsinki

167.5 Furi Furi

167.6 COLOURMOVIE

167.7 HandGun

167.8 inkgraphix

167.9 superfamous

168.1 the brainbox

168.2 zookeeper

168.3 the brainbox

168.4 canefantasma studio

168.5 tokidoki

168.6 Tsuyoshi Hirooka

168.7 the brainbox

168.8 REGINA

169.1 viagrafik

169.2 viagrafik

169.3 Nonstop

169.4 Vår

169.5 Mark Sloan

FASHION

MODE

Brands and products, shops and boutiques, shows and other events: how designers translate design-related fashion into symbols – this chapter shows a broad and varied spectrum on that.

Marken und Produkte, Geschäfte und Boutiquen, Messen und andere Events: Wie Gestalter das design-verwandte Thema Mode in Zeichen umsetzen – davon zeigt dieses Kapitel ein buntes und breites Spektrum.

RINZEN

"FEAR AND RESPECT THE GOOD LOGO, YE BLIGHTED SINNERS!"

Where do you get inspiration for your work?
From our Planet Earth and all good creatures that gambol on it.

Do you work according to a definite design philosophy?
Rinzen prefers a post-ironic, post-pastoral, post-humorist approach to visual design. We try to be light-hearted and cheerful, but not ironic, spontaneous but not indiscriminate; to integrate but not to derive.

What would you say is the key to a good, successful logo?
A good logo is independent, characterful and timeless. It carries the weight of its identity convincingly and indivisibly. The Good Logo does not ask for goodwill and sympathy and shows no mercy; it is the punishing iron fist of typographical law. Fear and respect the Logo, ye blighted sinners! ... A great logo is all that, as soon as our invoice has been paid.

Do your aesthetic values and your clients' demands ever clash?
There should not be aesthetic clashes between a serious client and a professional designer that add up to more than those between air and breathing. Anyone who acts differently is a con man who should be put in the stocks and despised for his crass behaviour.

If a client wasn't prepared to accept your work, how far would you be prepared to compromise?
We'll let you know if it ever happens.

Wo holt ihr euch die Inspirationen für eure Arbeit?
Von unserem Planeten Erde und allen guten Geschöpfen, die sich darauf tummeln.

Arbeitet ihr nach einer definierten Designphilosophie?
Rinzen bevorzugt eine post-ironische, post-pastorale, post-humoristische Annäherungsweise an die visuelle Gestaltung. Wir bemühen uns heiter und fröhlich, aber nicht ironisch; spontan, aber nicht wahllos zu sein – zu integrieren, aber nicht abzuleiten.

Was charakterisiert in euren Augen ein gutes, ein gelungenes Logo?
Ein gutes Logo ist eigenständig, charakteristisch und zeitlos. Es trägt das Gewicht seiner Identität überzeugend und unteilbar. Das Gute Logo bittet nicht um Wohlwollen oder Sympathie und gewährt keine Gnade; es ist die strafende eiserne Faust des typographischen Gesetzes. Fürchtet und respektiert das Logo, ihr verblendeten Sünder! ... Ein großes Logo ist all das, sobald unsere Rechnung bezahlt worden ist.

Gibt's Konflikte zwischen euren ästhetischen Wertvorstellungen und den Ansprüchen eurer Kunden?
Es sollte keine größeren ästhetischen Konflikte zwischen einem ernsthaften Kunden und einem professionellen Designer geben als zwischen der Luft und dem Atmen. Jeder, der anders agiert, ist ein Betrüger, der für sein ungeschliffenes Verhalten an den Pranger gestellt und verachtet werden sollte.

Angenommen, ein Kunde akzeptiert eure Arbeit nicht: Wie weit lasst ihr euch dann auf Kompromisse ein?
Wir lassen's euch wissen, falls das je passieren sollte.

RINZEN, New Farm, Queensland, Australia | www.rinzen.com

RINZEN, New Farm, Queensland, Australien | www.rinzen.com

172.1 weissraum

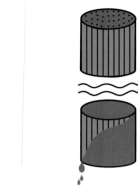

172.2 Rob Abeyta

172.3 Rob Abeyta

172.4 Rob Abeyta

172.5 Peter Vattanatham

172.6 Zion Graphics

172.7 POWER GRAPHIXX

172.8 KEEP LEFT STUDIO

172.9 Nendo Graphic Squad

172.10 Nobody

172.11 Rob Abeyta

172.12 KEEP LEFT STUDIO

173.1 bleed

173.2 Gianni Rossi

173.3 Gianni Rossi

173.4 struggle inc

173.5 New Future People

174.1 incorect

174.2 incorect

174.3 incorect

174.4 incorect

174.5 Nendo Graphic Squad

174.6 stylodesign

174.7 lindedesign

174.8 a+morph

174.9 polygraph

174.10 Masa Colectivo Gráfico

174.11 POWER GRAPHIXX

174.12 ohiogirl Design

174.13 NULLPROZENTFETT

174.14 Tsuyoshi Kusano

174.15 POWER GRAPHIXX

174.16 POWER GRAPHIXX

175.1 Io Design

175.2 Io Design

175.3 Rob Abeyta

175.4 viagrafik

175.5 Carsten Raffel

175.6 OCKTAK

175.7 tokidoki

175.8 Io Design

175.9 automatic art & design

175.10 KEEP LEFT STUDIO

175.11 Jorge Alderete

175.12 weissraum

175.13 jum

175.14 lindedesign

175.15 Parra

175.16 Parra

176.1 Chris Hutchinson   176.2 Chris Hutchinson   176.3 weissraum

JimStyle™

177.1 weissraum

177.2 weissraum

177.3 BORDFUNK

•

178.1 POWER GRAPHIXX

178.2 Zion Graphics

178.3 tokidoki

178.4 Parra

178.5 Parra

178.6 Rob Abeyta

179.1 tokidoki

179.2 tokidoki

179.3 tokidoki

179.4 tokidoki

179.5 tokidoki

179.6 ala webstatt

179.7 tokidoki

179.8 tokidoki

179.9 tokidoki

179.10 tokidoki

179.11 tokidoki

179.12 tokidoki

180.1 Happypets Products

180.2 Masa Colectivo Gráfico

180.3 Zion Graphics

180.4 Happypets Products

180.5 Masa Colectivo Gráfico

180.6 Zion Graphics

181.1 Tsuyoshi Hirooka

181.2 Zion Graphics

181.3 polygraph

181.4 Tsuyoshi Hirooka

181.5 Zion Graphics

181.6 polygraph

182.1 Happypets Products

182.2 Happypets Products

182.3 Happypets Products

182.4 Happypets Products

182.5 Happypets Products

182.6 Happypets Products

183.1 Happypets Products

183.2 Masa Colectivo Gráfico

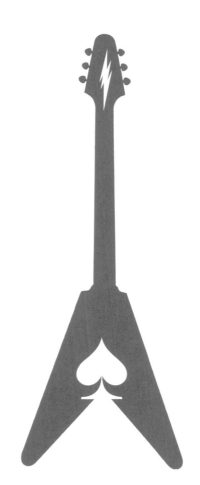

183.3 Masa Colectivo Gráfico

183.4 Formgeber

184.1 incorect

184.2 incorect

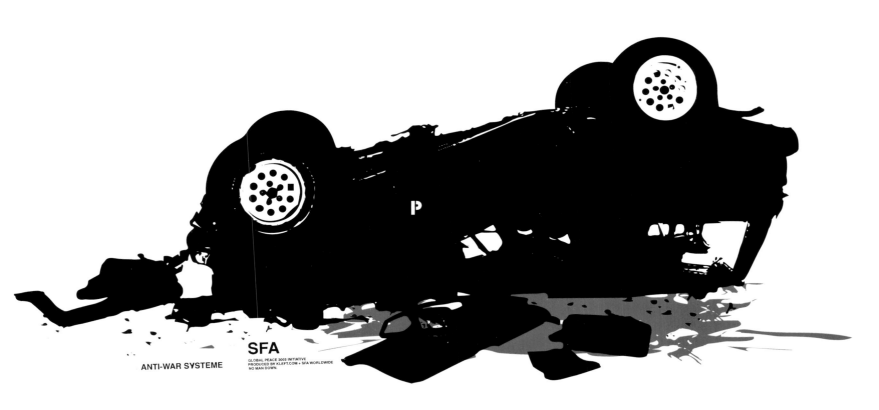

ANTI-WAR SYSTEME

SFA
GLOBAL PEACE 2003 INITIATIVE
PRODUCED BY KLEFT.COM + SFA WORLDWIDE
NO MAN DOWN.

185.1 KEEP LEFT STUDIO

186.1 Parra

186.2 Parra

186.3 Tsuyoshi Hirooka

186.4 KEEP LEFT STUDIO

186.5 nu designs+ yanku

186.6 viagrafik

186.7 Finsta

186.8 Nobody

186.9 everyday icons

/AFK

186.10 Tsuyoshi Hirooka

186.11 VASAVA

186.12 Carsten Raffel

187.1 Vår

187.2 Vår

187.3 Chris Hutchinson

187.4 Io Design

187.5 Tsuyoshi Hirooka

187.6 Rob Abeyta

187.7 Zion Graphics

187.8 KEEP LEFT STUDIO

187.9 Parra

187.10 Tsuyoshi Hirooka

187.11 Furi Furi

187.12 Vår

188.1 FUTRO

188.2 doublestandards

188.3 Nobody

188.4 FROZT

188.5 Niels Jansson

188.6 Peter Vattanatham

188.7 Nobody

188.8 ohiogirl Design

189.1 Nendo Graphic Squad

189.2 Tsuyoshi Hirooka

189.3 Nendo Graphic Squad

189.4 Tsuyoshi Hirooka

189.5 POWER GRAPHIXX

189.6 Tsuyoshi Hirooka

189.7 wuff design

189.8 Tsuyoshi Hirooka

190.1 KEEP LEFT STUDIO

190.2 Rinzen

190.3 Rinzen

190.4 KEEP LEFT STUDIO

190.5 Rinzen

190.6 KEEP LEFT STUDIO

190.7 Rinzen

190.8 KEEP LEFT STUDIO

190.9 Nonstop

190.10 ohiogirl Design

190.11 METHOD

190.12 POWER GRAPHIXX

190.13 Max Henschel

190.14 BÜRO DESTRUCT

190.15 Niels Jansson

190.16 everyday icons

191.1 everyday icons

191.2 no-domain

191.3 no-domain

191.4 Syrup Helsinki

191.5 Tsuyoshi Hirooka

191.6 KEEP LEFT STUDIO

191.7 KEEP LEFT STUDIO

191.8 POWER GRAPHIXX

191.9 KEEP LEFT STUDIO

191.10 KEEP LEFT STUDIO

191.11 BlackJune

191.12 Tsuyoshi Hirooka

191.13 POWER GRAPHIXX

191.14 POWER GRAPHIXX

191.15 Tsuyoshi Hirooka

191.16 POWER GRAPHIXX

192.1 Parra

192.2 Parra

192.3 Parra

192.4 Parra

192.5 Parra

192.6 Parra

192.7 Parra

192.8 Deanne Cheuk

192.9 Zion Graphics

192.10 Parra

192.11 Syrup Helsinki

192.12 Kingsize

192.13 J6Studios

192.14 Hula Hula

192.15 Digitalultras

192.16 Hort

193.1 Deanne Cheuk

193.2 Planet Pixel

193.3 dmote

193.4 struggle inc

194.1 Kallegraphics

194.2 weissraum

194.3 Zion Graphics

194.4 Chris Hutchinson

194.5 A-Side Studio

194.6 Planet Pixel

194.7 automatic art & design

195.1 KEEP LEFT STUDIO

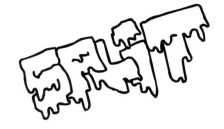

195.2 KEEP LEFT STUDIO

195.3 KEEP LEFT STUDIO

195.4 KEEP LEFT STUDIO

195.5 KEEP LEFT STUDIO

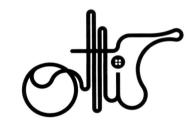

195.6 no-domain

195.7 no-domain

195.8 ohiogirl Design

195.9 ohiogirl Design

196.1 Parra

196.2 Balsi Grafik

196.3 weissraum

196.4 shida keiichi design

196.5 bleed

196.6 Carsten Raffel

196.7 BÜRO DESTRUCT

196.8 Rinzen

196.9 tokidoki

196.10 Nobody

196.11 weissraum

196.12 Vår

196.13 Parra

196.14 eboy

196.15 Gianni Rossi

196.16 Digitalultras

Kinky Dirty

Manuel and Juny
Dirty Hands .

197.1 Digitalultras

198.1 stylodesign

198.2 bleed

198.3 GWG CO. LTD

198.4 Formgeber

198.5 Tsuyoshi Kusano

198.6 KEEP LEFT STUDIO

198.7 KEEP LEFT STUDIO

198.8 ohiogirl Design

198.9 GWG CO. LTD

198.10 ala webstatt

198.11 Parra

198.12 viagrafik

198.13 BlackJune

198.14 Zion Graphics

198.15 TAK!

198.16 Tsuyoshi Hirooka

199.1 polygraph

199.2 BÜRO DESTRUCT

199.3 Chris Hutchinson

199.4 Syrup Helsinki

199.5 bleed

199.6 POWER GRAPHIXX

199.7 Formgeber

199.8 Gianni Rossi

199.9 Nendo Graphic Squad

199.10 Nendo Graphic Squad

199.11 J6Studios

199.12 BlackJune

199.13 Maniackers Design

199.14 blindresearch

199.15 everyday icons

199.16 Niels Jansson

200.1 Syrup Helsinki

200.2 Gianni Rossi

200.3 zookeeper

200.4 HandGun

200.5 Jorge Alderete

201.1 KEEP LEFT STUDIO

201.2 KEEP LEFT STUDIO

201.3 everyday icons

201.4 KEEP LEFT STUDIO

201.5 Digitalultras

201.6 POWER GRAPHIXX

202.1 New Future People

202.2 New Future People

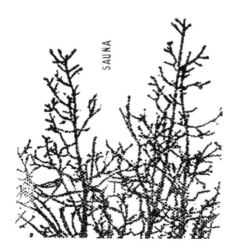

202.3 Tina Backman

202.4 Masa Colectivo Gráfico

203.1 Masa Colectivo Gráfico

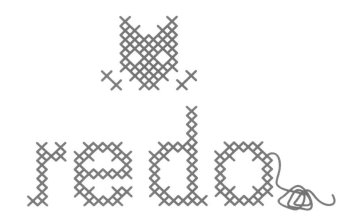

203.2 rubber type citizens

203.3 everyday icons

203.4 automatic art & design

204.1 KEEP LEFT STUDIO

204.2 New Future People

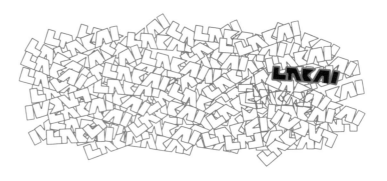

204.3 ohiogirl Design

205.1 fupete studio

205.2 KEEP LEFT STUDIO

205.3 KEEP LEFT STUDIO

205.4 Positron

206.1 Zion Graphics

206.2 Zion Graphics

206.3 Zion Graphics

206.4 Zion Graphics

206.5 Zion Graphics

206.6 Zion Graphics

206.7 KEEP LEFT STUDIO

206.8 Digitalultras

206.9 KEEP LEFT STUDIO

207.1 Masa Colectivo Gráfico

207.2 Masa Colectivo Gráfico

207.3 Masa Colectivo Gráfico

207.4 the brainbox

207.5 KEEP LEFT STUDIO

207.6 KEEP LEFT STUDIO

207.7 HandGun

207.8 Masa Colectivo Gráfico

207.9 Nendo Graphic Squad

208.1 automatic art & design

208.2 struggle inc

208.3 polygraph

208.4 ohiogirl Design

208.5 Finsta

208.6 HandGun

208.7 Formgeber

208.8 BlackJune

208.9 POWER GRAPHIXX

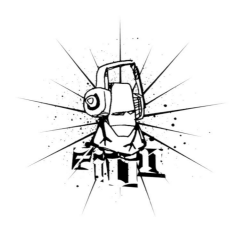

209.1 Zion Graphics

209.2 Zion Graphics

209.3 Zion Graphics

209.4 Zion Graphics

209.5 Zion Graphics

209.6 Masa Colectivo Gráfico

210.1 BlackJune

210.2 Meomi Design

210.3 ohiogirl Design

210.4 Rob Abeyta

210.5 New Future People

210.6 POWER GRAPHIXX

210.7 POWER GRAPHIXX

210.8 Zion Graphics

210.9 KEEP LEFT STUDIO

210.10 phunk

210.11 weissraum

210.12 struggle inc

210.13 Masa Colectivo Gráfico

210.14 Masa Colectivo Gráfico

210.15 Masa Colectivo Gráfico

210.16 Masa Colectivo Gráfico

211.1 tokidoki

211.2 HandGun

211.3 weissraum

211.4 Furi Furi

211.5 Parra

211.6 Digitalultras

211.7 dopepope

211.8 dopepope

211.9 Carsten Raffel

211.10 Karlssonwilker Inc.

211.11 phunk

211.12 Rob Abeyta

211.13 Tsuyoshi Hirooka

211.14 Carsten Raffel

211.15 Carsten Raffel

211.16 vektor 3

212.1 the brainbox

212.2 Vår

212.3 incorect

212.4 the brainbox

212.5 Meomi Design

212.6 BlackJune

213.1 no-domain

213.2 Parra

213.3 ohiogirl Design

213.4 Parra

213.5 KEEP LEFT STUDIO

214.1 nu designs+ yanku

214.2 Rob Abeyta

214.3 MAGNETOFONICA

214.4 Planet Pixel

214.5 Hula Hula

214.6 Gianni Rossi

214.7 Gianni Rossi

214.8 Gianni Rossi

214.9 Nobody

214.10 automatic art & design

214.11 plumnotion

214.12 automatic art & design

214.13 Maniackers Design

214.14 automatic art & design

214.15 zookeeper

214.16 sunrise studios

215.1 A´

215.2 B.ü.L.b grafix

215.3 GWG CO. LTD

215.4 Nobody

215.5 Um-bruch

215.6 zookeeper

215.7 Masa Colectivo Gráfico

215.8 Lisa Schibel

215.9 Sebastian Gerbert

215.10 everyday icons

215.11 310 K

215.12 viagrafik

215.13 Nendo Graphic Squad

215.14 Nobody

215.15 POWER GRAPHIXX

215.16 Nobody

216.1 KEEP LEFT STUDIO

216.2 KEEP LEFT STUDIO

216.3 Nobody

216.4 Furi Furi

216.5 Masa Colectivo Gráfico

216.6 Zion Graphics

216.7 Gianni Rossi

216.8 automatic art & design

216.9 Formgeber

217.1 Furi Furi

217.2 Furi Furi

217.3 Positron

217.4 Masa Colectivo Gráfico

217.5 automatic art & design

217.6 Digitalultras

218.1 Masa Colectivo Gráfico

218.2 Meomi Design

218.3 Meomi Design

218.4 Meomi Design

218.5 Meomi Design

218.6 Meomi Design

218.7 Furi Furi

219.1 Furi Furi

219.2 tokidoki

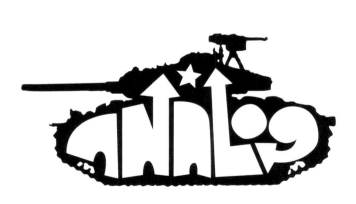

219.3 struggle inc

219.4 struggle inc

*

220.1 Planet Pixel

220.2 zookeeper

220.3 Zion Graphics

220.4 Zion Graphics

220.5 Parra

220.6 forcefeed:swede

221.1 ohiogirl Design

221.2 ohiogirl Design

221.3 Parra

221.4 Rinzen

221.5 Rinzen

221.6 Rinzen

222.2 Rinzen

222.1 Rinzen

222.3 Rinzen

222.4 Chris Hutchinson

223.1 Rinzen

IN MOTION
GAMES

IN MOTION
GAMES

This chapter is driven by action and movement. Logos reflecting the typical character of computer and video games. Pictograms and figures for another world – that of the Global Game Community. Demonstrations of logo development processes provide a second focus for this chapter.

Dieses Kapitel wird durch Aktion und Bewegung geprägt. Logos, die den typischen Charakter der Computer- und Videospiele reflektieren. Piktogramme und Figuren für eine andere Welt – die der globalen Game-Community. Demonstrationen von Logoentwicklungs-Prozessen bilden einen zweiten Schwerpunkt dieses Kapitels.

MK 12

"MOST OF ALL ENJOYMENT IS IMPORTANT."

Where do you get inspiration for your work?
Anything that's a bit shabby, kitschy, scruffy inspires us. Especially things that go into our scanner. We're inspired by video cassettes we ferret out in videotheque stock, the soundtracks of old action movies, knotted, Mid-Western macramé stuff, the many amazing things you can find in flea-markets. We are inspired by science, by physics, even though we don't understand a lot about it. Truckers' joints and kerb-cruising areas are our museums. Oh yes, and of course we're inspired by the breath-taking variety of the natural world with all the little creatures that creep and peep there.

Do you work according to a definite design philosophy?
You can scarcely afford a philosophy today. But it would also be wrong to say that we would just produce any old thing. There is still another side to it all. It's true we're really stubborn about a lot of things, but everything goes all right after a really good meeting. We are workaholics, but hellishly lazy ones. Balance is important, independence is important, but having fun with things is most important. Huge quantities of coffee aren't bad either.

What would you say is the key to a good, successful logo?
Good – and great – logos usually have animals or strange characters built in. The Japanese are in no doubt about that, and it's no secret to Sinclair Oil.

Do your aesthetic values and your clients' demands ever clash?
When it comes to clashes we behave the same as our State Attorney Richard Ashcroft. We consistently insist on, even impose all our values, whether it makes sense in the individual case or not. That applies to shareholders, agencies and anyone we deal with. And if it happens not to work out in the end we bring in people whose job is to clear things like that up. Our production team is very, very diplomatic. But we can't help our crude behaviour, it's in out blood. Our ancestors were bloodthirsty, Mongol-type mad Vikings from Alabama, so there's nothing you can do about it...

If a client wasn't prepared to accept your work, how far would you be prepared to compromise?
We do what we have to do to get a job finished. What else are we supposed to do? It's sometimes difficult working with people you can't get any positive response from. But as a pro you can't just chuck an unfinished project. But that doesn't mean we don't risk expressing our opinions clearly. But still, yes, we do compromise, very often, more often than we'd actually like.

mk 12, Kansas City, USA | www.mk 12.com

Wo holt ihr euch die Inspirationen für eure Arbeit?
Alles, was ein bisschen schäbig, kitschig, abgenutzt ist, inspiriert uns. Speziell Sachen, die in unseren Scanner gehen. Wir lassen uns von VHS-Kassetten inspirieren, die wir in den Lagern von Videotheken aufstöbern, von Soundtracks aus alten Action-Filmen, von geknüpften Midwestern Makramee-Sachen, von der Fülle an merkwürdigen Dingen, die sich auf Flohmärkten entdecken lassen. Wir sind inspiriert von der Wissenschaft, der Physik, obwohl wir nicht viel davon verstehen. Truckfahrer-Treffpunkte und der Straßenstrich sind unsere Museen. Oh ja, und natürlich inspiriert uns die atemberaubende Vielfalt der natürlichen Welt mit allen Kreaturen, die darauf kreuchen und fleuchen.

Arbeitet ihr nach einer definierten Designphilosophie?
Man kann es sich heutzutage kaum mehr leisten, eine Philosophie zu haben. In manchen Situationen sind wir wirklich hartnäckig. Wir sind Workaholics, aber mit einem höllischen Hang zur Trägheit. Ausgeglichenheit ist wichtig, Unabhängigkeit ist wichtig, aber vor allem wichtig ist der Spaß an der Sache. Unmengen von Kaffee sind auch nicht schlecht.

Was charakterisiert in euren Augen ein gutes, ein gelungenes Logo?
In guten – und großen – Logos sind meistens Tiere oder komische Typen integriert. Den Japanern ist das völlig klar, und auch für Sinclair Oil ist das kein Geheimnis.

Gibt's Konflikte zwischen euren ästhetischen Wertvorstellungen und den Ansprüchen eurer Kunden?
Was Konflikte angeht, so machen wir's wie unser Justizminister Richard Ashcroft. Wir sind so konsequent, allen unsere Werte aufzuerlegen, vielmehr aufzunötigen, ob's nun im Einzelfall sinnvoll ist oder nicht. Das betrifft Aktionäre, Agenturen und alle, mit denen wir es zu tun haben. Wenn das dann schlussendlich nicht aufgehen sollte, dann ziehen wir Leute hinzu, deren Job es ist, solche Fragen zu klären. Unser Produktionsteam ist sehr, sehr diplomatisch. Aber wir selbst können nichts für unser rüdes Benehmen, es liegt uns im Blut. Unsere Vorfahren waren nämlich blutdürstige, mongolenartige, verrückte Wikinger aus Alabama, da kann man nichts machen...

Angenommen, ein Kunde akzeptiert eure Arbeit nicht: Wie weit lasst ihr euch dann auf Kompromisse ein?
Gelegentlich ist es schwierig, mit Leuten zu arbeiten, von denen kein positives Echo kommt. Aber als Profi kannst du ein nicht abgeschlossenes Projekt nicht einfach so hinschmeißen. Das heißt aber nicht, dass wir uns nicht das Recht herausnehmen klar unsere Meinung zu sagen. Ja, wir machen Kompromisse, öfter als wir eigentlich wollen.

mk 12, Kansas City, USA | www.mk 12.com

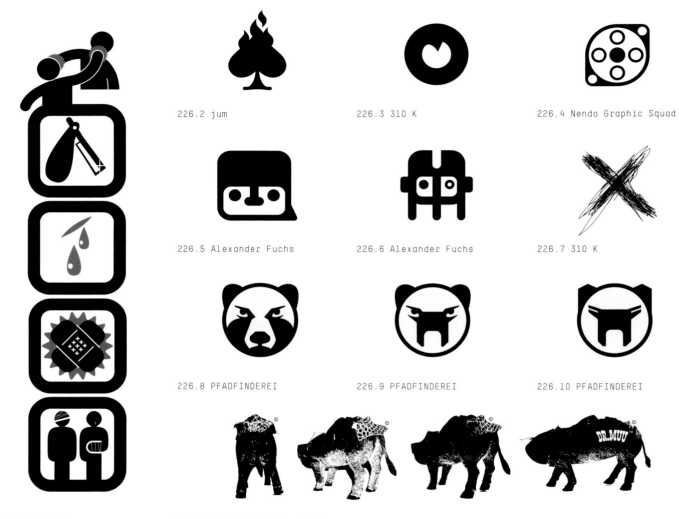

226.2 jum

226.3 310 K

226.4 Nendo Graphic Squad

226.5 Alexander Fuchs

226.6 Alexander Fuchs

226.7 310 K

226.8 PFADFINDEREI

226.9 PFADFINDEREI

226.10 PFADFINDEREI

226.1 incorect

226.11 Masa Colectivo Gráfico

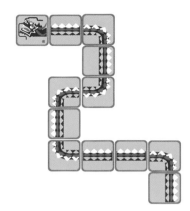

227.1 tokidoki

227.2 tokidoki

227.3 tokidoki

227.4 tokidoki

227.5 tokidoki

227.6 MK12 Design Studio

227.7 tokidoki

227.8 tokidoki

227.9 Meomi Design

227.10 MK12 Design Studio

227.11 tokidoki

228.1 MK12 Design Studio

228.2 MK12 Design Studio

228.3 MK12 Design Studio

228.4 Peter Vattanatham

228.5 310 K

228.6 PLEIX

228.7 jum

228.8 polygraph

228.9 Parra

228.10 no-domain

228.11 PLEIX

228.12 doublestandards

228.13 PLEIX

228.14 PLEIX

228.13 PLEIX

228.14 PLEIX

228.15 WEWORKFORTHEM

228.16 WEWORKFORTHEM

229.1 NULLPROZENTFETT

229.2 polygraph

229.3 Tsuyoshi Kusano

229.4 Tsuyoshi Kusano

229.5 PLEIX

229.6 Tsuyoshi Hirooka

230.1 MK12 Design Studio

230.2 MK12 Design Studio

230.3 MK12 Design Studio

230.4 MK12 Design Studio

230.5 Parra

230.6 Parra

230.7 MK12 Design Studio

230.8 MK12 Design Studio

230.9 MK12 Design Studio

230.10 MK12 Design Studio

230.11 MK12 Design Studio

230.12 MK12 Design Studio

230.13 Parra

230.14 Parra

230.15 KEEP LEFT STUDIO

230.16 COLOURMOVIE

231.1 Kingsize

231.2 MK12 Design Studio

231.3 MK12 Design Studio

231.4 MK12 Design Studio

231.5 MK12 Design Studio

231.6 MK12 Design Studio

231.7 MK12 Design Studio

231.8 MK12 Design Studio

232.1 MK12 Design Studio

232.2 MK12 Design Studio

232.3 chemical box

232.4 Parra

233.1 Peter Vattanatham

233.2 WEWORKFORTHEM

233.3 MK12 Design Studio

233.4 Nendo Graphic Squad

234.1 Raum Mannheim

234.2 Masa Colectivo Gráfico

234.3 Masa Colectivo Gráfico

234.4 Tsuyoshi Kusano

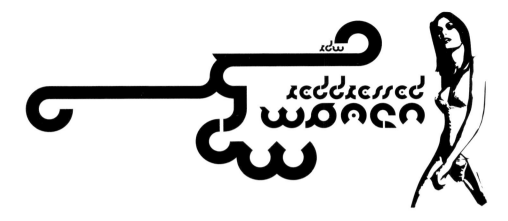

235.1 NULLPROZENTFETT

235.2 A'   235.3 NULLPROZENTFETT   235.4 Tsuyoshi Hirooka

236.1 tokidoki

236.2 tokidoki

236.3 everyday icons

236.4 Kingsize

236.5 jum

236.6 viagrafik

236.7 Miguel Angel Leyva

236.8 COLOURMOVIE

237.1 Parra

237.2 MK12 Design Studio

RHIZOME

By visiting rhizome.org, your current IP address and the IP addresses of the last three visitors are determined.

Next, the four numbers in each IP address are added together.
The digits of the resulting number are added together consecutively until a single digit is reached:

216.179.13.35 = 443
4 + 4 + 3 = 11
1 + 1 = 2
2

This single number is compared to the following special color chart:

After the color is selected, the IP address is plotted in a star shape. each of the four numbers in the IP address corresponds to a line in the star.
The position of the line is measured in degrees starting counter-clockwise from the 'three o'clock' position. A number of '90' will point due north, a number of '240' will point southwest, and so on like this:

216.179.13.35   24.64.71.160   149.166.232.102   152.3.28.191

Finally, the four stars are superimposed to create the final logo design.

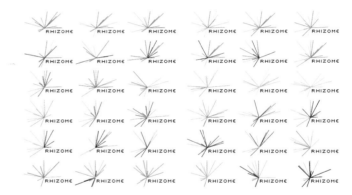

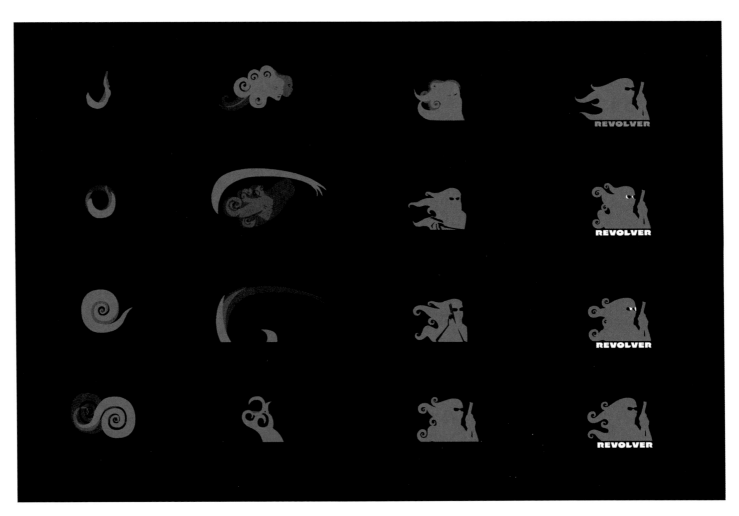

239.1 Gianni Rossi

MEDIA

MEDIA

This chapter reflects the heterogeneous nature of our media world and presents numerous example of how and with what creative devices figures from the current designer scene find appropriate and memorable symbols for TV stations and magazines, websites, radio stations and other media.

Dieses Kapitel reflektiert den heterogenen Charakter unserer Medienwelt, und zeigt an zahlreichen Beispielen, wie und mit welchen Gestaltungselementen Vertreter der aktuellen Designerszene für TV-Sender und Zeitschriften, Websites, Radiostationen und andere Medien adäquate und einprägsame Zeichen setzen.

TSUYOSHI HIROOKA

"I CAN ONLY CREATE MY WORK FROM THE SENSE THAT I HAVE INSIDE OF ME."

Where do you get inspiration for your work?
Sometimes the idea comes from what a logo symbolizes, what it stands for; sometimes when I look at a sequence of characters.

Do you work according to a definite design philosophy?
It has its good side and its bad side, but I like to keep my philosophy in a permanent state of change as a matter of principle. At the moment I am more focused on creating atmosphere and less on pursuing fixed, completed forms.

What would you say is the key to a good, successful logo?
A pioneering idea that comes out of sleepless nights and a relaxed approach to realising it when I have slept well.

Do your aesthetic values and your clients' demands ever clash?
It depends on the client. If I see there is a clash I explain my values to them and try to understand theirs.

If a client wasn't prepared to accept your work, how far would you be prepared to compromise?
I can only create my work from the sense that I have inside of me. Of course I try to understand the client's feelings as well. Somehow that has always worked so far. I think it's more to do with making an effort than about compromise.

Wo holst du dir die Inspirationen für deine Arbeit?
Manchmal kommt die Idee von dem, was ein Logo symbolisiert, für was es steht; manchmal, wenn ich eine Abfolge von Typen betrachte.

Arbeitest du nach einer definierten Designphilosophie?
Obwohl das eine gute und eine schlechte Seite hat, möchte ich grundsätzlich die Philosophie in einem permanenten Veränderungsprozess halten. Im Moment bin ich mehr darauf fokussiert, Atmosphäre zu schaffen und weniger darauf, festgelegte, fertige Formen zu verfolgen.

Was charakterisiert in deinen Augen ein gutes, ein gelungenes Logo?
Eine bahnbrechende Idee, die in schlaflosen Nächten entsteht und ein lockeres Herangehen an die Realisierung, wenn ich ausgeschlafen bin.

Gibt's Konflikte zwischen euren ästhetischen Wertvorstellungen und den Ansprüchen eurer Kunden?
Das kommt auf den Kunden an. Wenn ich einen Konflikt erkenne, erkläre ich ihm zuerst meine Wertvorstellungen und versuche dann seine zu begreifen.

Angenommen, ein Kunde akzeptiert deine Arbeit nicht: Wie weit lässt du dich dann auf Kompromisse ein?
Meine kreative Arbeit wächst aus dem Gefühl, das ich in mir habe. Ich bemühe mich natürlich auch die Gefühle des Kunden zu verstehen. Irgendwie hat das bisher immer funktioniert. Ich glaube, das hat eher etwas mit sich bemühen zu tun als mit Kompromissen.

Tsuyoshi Hirooka, Tokyo, Japan | hiro-ka.serveftp.com

Tsuyoshi Hirooka, Tokio, Japan | hiro-ka.serveftp.com

•

242.1 WEWORKFORTHEM

242.2 WEWORKFORTHEM

242.3 Positron

242.4 WEWORKFORTHEM

242.5 WEWORKFORTHEM

242.6 Nonstop

242.7 310 K

242.8 ZIP Design

242.9 Sebastian Gerbert

242.10 Tsuyoshi Hirooka

242.11 Tsuyoshi Hirooka

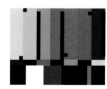

242.12 no-domain

243.1 Alexander Fuchs

243.2 WG Berlin

243.3 Digitalultras

243.4 Tsuyoshi Kusano

243.5 Alexander Fuchs

243.6 Alexander Fuchs

243.7 Felix Braden

243.8 Alexander Fuchs

243.9 Formgeber

243.10 Formgeber

243.11 Formgeber

243.12 Formgeber

244.1 Positron

244.2 phunk

244.3 jum

244.4 POWER GRAPHIXX

244.5 Positron

244.6 phunk

245.1 Gozer Media

245.2 FUTRO

245.3 Formgeber

245.4 everyday icons

245.5 A-Side Studio

245.6 Formgeber

246.1 Balsi Grafik

246.2 weissraum

246.3 Tsuyoshi Kusano

246.4 Kallegraphics

246.5 Kallegraphics

246.6 Kallegraphics

246.7 no-domain

246.8 bleed

246.9 Masa Colectivo Gráfico

247.1 sweaterweather

247.2 Rinzen

247.3 mikati

247.4 mikati

247.5 KEEP LEFT STUDIO

247.6 EBOY

247.7 everyday icons

247.8 WEWORKFORTHEM

247.9 Digitalultras

248.1 viagrafik

248.2 viagrafik

248.3 viagrafik

248.4 viagrafik

248.5 viagrafik

248.6 KEEP LEFT STUDIO

248.7 sweaterweather

248.8 sweaterweather

248.9 sweaterweather

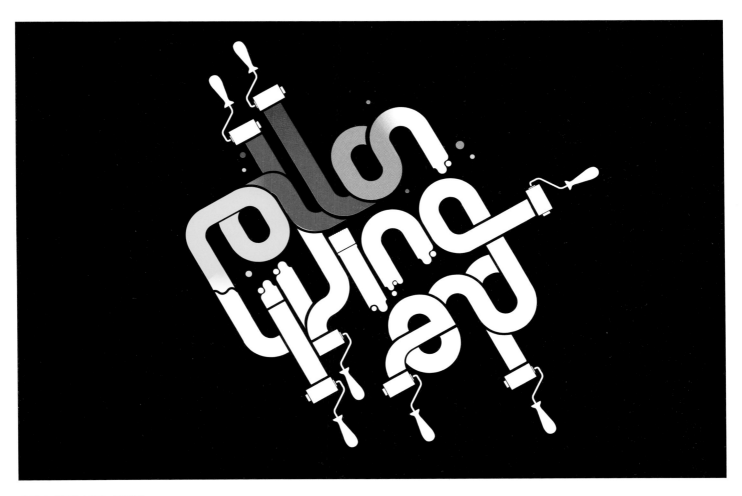

249.1 KEEP LEFT STUDIO

250.1 KEEP LEFT STUDIO

250.2 no-domain

250.3 Genevieve Gauckler

250.4 no-domain

250.5 everyday icons

250.6 everyday icons

251.1 Jürgen und ich

251.2 struggle inc

251.3 Balsi Grafik

251.4 WEWORKFORTHEM

251.5 automatic art & design

251.6 WEWORKFORTHEM

251.7 BORDFUNK

251.8 Kallegraphics

252.1 Tsuyoshi Hirooka

252.2 Tsuyoshi Hirooka

252.3 Tsuyoshi Hirooka

252.4 Norm

252.5 Oscar Salinas Losada

252.6 Maniackers Design

252.7 VASAVA

252.8 weissraum

253.1 Zion Graphics

253.2 Superlow

253.3 Superlow

253.4 VASAVA

253.5 GWG CO. LTD

253.6 VASAVA

253.7 Planet Pixel

253.8 nothing medialab

Claudia

254.1 POWER GRAPHIXX

254.2 Oscar Salinas Losada

MONITOR

254.3 Tsuyoshi Kusano

PROJECT BROOKLYN

254.4 typotherapy

254.5 FUTRO

254.6 Tsuyoshi Hirooka

254.7 texelseboys & Artmiks

254.8 typotherapy

254.9 WEWORKFORTHEM

bigloader

255.1 stylodesign

circular

255.2 stylodesign

255.3 OCKTAK

255.4 Unit Delta Plus

255.5 plumnotion

255.6 lovelybrand

255.7 KEEP LEFT STUDIO

255.8 Rikus Hilmann

255.9 VASAVA

256.1 Nendo Graphic Squad

256.2 dmote

256.3 Nendo Graphic Squad

256.4 dmote

256.5 Digitalultras

256.6 Positron

256.7 Nendo Graphic Squad

256.8 J6Studios

256.9 Digitalultras

257.1 Tsuyoshi Hirooka

257.2 Nendo Graphic Squad

257.3 Maniackers Design

257.4 polygraph

257.5 Nendo Graphic Squad

257.6 POWER GRAPHIXX

257.7 Maniackers Design

デザインフレックス

258.1 Tsuyoshi Hirooka

ニンゲン、今日モ未チ味ク。

258.2 Tsuyoshi Hirooka

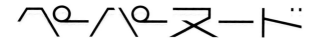

258.3 Tsuyoshi Hirooka

心理学批判社会

258.4 Tsuyoshi Kusano

258.5 Maniackers Design

気分はもう戦争2.1
PARACE QUE ES LA GUELLA 2.1 矢作俊彦×藤原カムイ
TOSHIHIKO YAHAGI × KAMUI FUJIWARA

258.6 Nendo Graphic Squad

258.7 Positron

交戦設想

258.8 Nendo Graphic Squad

SAL
洋楽
MANIA

259.1 Tsuyoshi Hirooka

緊急生捜査!
ガレッジ⊕
ハンティング
GALLEGE HUNTING THE URGENT INVESTIGATION

259.2 POWER GRAPHIXX

ニッポニアニッポン

259.3 Tsuyoshi Kusano

おとこ♂女★おんな♀男

259.4 Maniackers Design

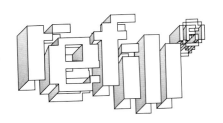

260.1 KEEP LEFT STUDIO

260.2 fupete studio

260.3 bleed

260.4 everyday icons

260.5 bleed

260.6 Chris Hutchinson

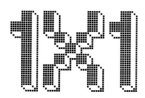

260.7 VASAVA

260.8 viagrafik

260.9 Maniackers Design

261.1 Maniackers Design

261.2 stylodesign

261.3 Planet Pixel

261.4 EBOY

261.5 Maniackers Design

261.6 Maniackers Design

262.1 Digitalultras

262.2 SWEDEN

262.3 Dubius?

262.4 no-domain

262.5 A-Side Studio

262.6 Masa Colectivo Gráfico

262.7 Jean-Jaques Tachdjian

262.8 Jean-Jaques Tachdjian

262.9 Jürgen und ich

263.1 Benjamin Güdel

263.2 Benjamin Güdel

263.3 Benjamin Güdel

263.4 Benjamin Güdel

263.5 Benjamin Güdel

263.6 Benjamin Güdel

263.7 Benjamin Güdel

263.8 Benjamin Güdel

FOUNDATION FOR ART & CREATIVE TECHNOLOGY

264.1 studiotonne

PROJECTS & TOURING

MITES

VIDEO POSITIVE

COLLABORATION PROGRAMME

264.2 studiotonne   264.3 studiotonne   264.4 studiotonne   264.5 studiotonne

265.1 Sanjai

265.2 Tsuyoshi Hirooka

265.3 stylodesign

265.4 Positron

265.5 BÜRO DESTRUCT

265.6 Kallegraphics

265.7 POWER GRAPHIXX

265.8 A-Side Studio

265.9 lovelybrand

265.10 A-Side Studio

265.11 Masa Colectivo Gráfico

265.12 POWER GRAPHIXX

265.13 FROZT

265.14 FROZT

265.15 zorglob

265.16 zorglob

266.1 Tsuyoshi Hirooka

266.2 VASAVA

266.3 struggle inc

266.4 bleed

266.5 WG Berlin

266.6 POWER GRAPHIXX

266.7 KEEP LEFT STUDIO

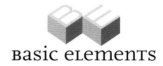

266.8 lovelybrand

266.9 VASAVA

266.10 zorglob

266.11 Hula Hula

266.12 zookeeper

266.13 VASAVA

266.14 no-domain

266.15 Casarramona

266.16 Maniackers Design

267.1 WG Berlin

267.2 Positron

267.3 A-Side Studio

267.4 strange//attraktor

267.5 WG Berlin

267.6 Meomi Design

267.7 zookeeper

267.8 struggle inc

267.9 BORDFUNK

267.10 POWER GRAPHIXX

267.11 sweaterweather

267.12 Syrup Helsinki

267.13 Maniackers Design

267.14 plumnotion

267.15 ZIP Design

267.16 superfamous

268.1 Formgeber

268.2 Tsuyoshi Hirooka

268.3 WG Berlin

268.4 Jean-Jaques Tachdjian

268.5 symbolodesign

268.6 Sanjai

268.7 viagrafik

268.8 Positron

268.9 VASAVA

268.10 METHOD

268.11 Axel Raidt

268.12 viagrafik

269.1 Benjamin Güdel

269.2 Masa Colectivo Gráfico

270.1 the brainbox

270.2 KEEP LEFT STUDIO

270.3 ZIP Design

270.4 Nonstop

270.5 Sanjai

270.6 VASAVA

270.7 KEEP LEFT STUDIO

270.8 struggle inc

270.9 weissraum

270.10 weissraum

270.11 weissraum

270.12 weissraum

271.1 316tn

271.2 Lisa Schibel

271.3 Cyclone Graphix

271.4 VASAVA

271.5 Felix Braden

271.6 Felix Braden

271.7 Felix Braden

271.8 viagrafik

271.9 Mark Sloan

271.10 POWER GRAPHIXX

271.11 jum

271.12 Yuu Imokawa

271.13 POWER GRAPHIXX

271.14 Maniackers Design

271.15 POWER GRAPHIXX

271.16 pictomat

272.1 zorglob

272.2 zorglob

272.3 POWER GRAPHIXX

272.4 viagrafik

272.5 Raum Mannheim

272.6 MetaDesign

272.7 chemical box

272.8 WG Berlin

272.9 POWER GRAPHIXX

272.10 weissraum

272.11 Digitalultras

272.12 viagrafik

272.13 316tn

273.1 incorect

273.2 incorect

273.3 ARK

273.4 WEWORKFORTHEM

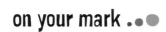

273.5 a small percent

273.6 Chris Hutchinson

273.7 FROZT

273.8 weissraum

273.9 Hanni Pannier

273.10 Maniackers Design

273.11 Jürgen und ich

273.12 viagrafik

273.13 sweaterweather

273.14 Masa Colectivo Gráfico

273.15 Masa Colectivo Gráfico

273.16 no-domain

274.1 St. Paulus Creative Force

274.2 KEEP LEFT STUDIO

274.3 HandGun

274.4 viagrafik

275.1 incorect

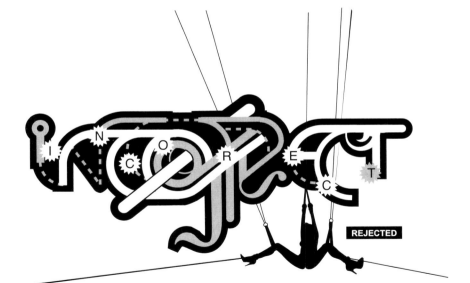

REJECTED

275.2 incorect

MUSIC

MUSIK

How do designers make the current music scene sing visually – music labels, groups, clubs, shops and festivals in various musical fields? This chapter shows some impressive responses.

Wie bringen Designer die aktuelle Musikszene, Musik-Labels, Bands, Clubs, Shops und Festivals aus vielen Musiksparten visuell zum Klingen? Dieses Kapitel zeigt repräsentative Antworten.

"SURTOUT PAS DE PHILOSOPHIE!"

Where do you get inspiration for your work?
From big multinationals' logos like Michelin, United Airlines, Warner Music, WWF, IBM ... or from the big groups, who are generally very effective and stable.

Do you work according to a definite design philosophy?
A philosophy? Please no! But we know our way about the most important basic forms.

What would you say is the key to a good, successful logo?
Good logos age well, and they are effective everywhere – it doesn't matter whether they're on a business card, an aircraft or a building.

Do your aesthetic values and your clients' demands ever clash?
Yes, there certainly are problems, especially in France, where clients don't have a graphic, visual culture at their fingertips to the same extent that the Anglo-Saxon countries do. Logos are over-intellectualised in France. The most important thing a logo has to do, representing a brand, can sometimes get forgotten. Often the client wants something completely new, without considering the laws of visibility, the effectiveness of the logo.

If a client wasn't prepared to accept your work, how far would you be prepared to compromise?
We usually do some research first to see what the client actually wants. We work with a particular end in sight, so that there aren't any nasty surprises at the end of the project. You have to let the client play some part in the creative process ... especially in France.

h5, Paris, France | www.h5.fr

Wo holt ihr euch die Inspirationen für eure Arbeit?
Von den Logos der großen, multinationalen Konzerne wie Michelin, United Airlines, Warner Music, WWF, IBM... oder von den großen Gruppen, die im Allgemeinen sehr wirkungsvoll und stabil sind.

Arbeitet ihr nach einer definierten Designphilosophie?
Eine Philosophie? Bloß nicht! Aber wir kennen uns aus in den wichtigsten Grundformen.

Was charakterisiert in euren Augen ein gutes, ein gelungenes Logo?
Gute Logos bleiben mit ihrem Alter immer gut, und sie wirken überall – egal, ob sie auf einer Visitenkarte, einem Flugzeug oder einem Gebäude appliziert sind.

Gibt's Konflikte zwischen euren ästhetischen Wertvorstellungen und den Ansprüchen eurer Kunden?
Ja, da gibt's sehr wohl Probleme, vor allem in Frankreich, wo die Kunden nicht in dem Maße über eine grafische, visuelle Kultur verfügen wie in den angelsächsischen Ländern. In Frankreich wird das Logo zu sehr intellektualisiert. Die wichtigste Funktion, die ein Logo zu erfüllen hat – nämlich eine Marke zu repräsentieren – wird dabei manchmal vergessen. Oft will der Kunde etwas völlig Neues, ohne Rücksicht auf die Regeln der Visibilität, der Wirksamkeit des Logos.

Angenommen, ein Kunde akzeptiert eure Arbeit nicht: Wie weit lasst ihr euch dann auf Kompromisse ein?
Im Allgemeinen recherchieren wir zuerst um herauszufinden, wohin der Kunde will. Wir arbeiten zielgerichtet, damit es am Schluss des Projektes keine bösen Überraschungen gibt. Man muss den Kunden am kreativen Prozess teilhaben lassen... vor allem in Frankreich.

h5, Paris, Frankreich | www.h5.fr

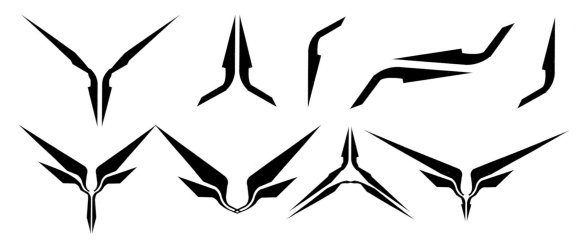

278.1 KEEP LEFT STUDIO

278.2 doublestandards

278.3 H5

278.4 3 Particles

278.5 310 K

278.6 KEEP LEFT STUDIO

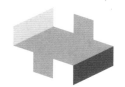

278.7 studiotonne

278.8 MK12 Design Studio

278.9 MK12 Design Studio

60	61	62	63	64	65	66	67	68	69	70	71	72	73	74	75	76	77	78	79
					mosz	⌐	⌐	⌐	⌐	⌐	(	⌐	⌐	~	⌐	⌐	mosz	)	mosz
80	81	82	83	84	85	86	87	88	89	90	91	92	93	94	95	96	97	98	99
⌐	~	~	mosz	(	(	(	)	⌐	~	mosz							mosz		

mosz

⌐

279.1 re-p

279.2 Superlow

280.2 weissraum

280.3 Rikus Hilmann

280.4 raster-noton

280.5 WEWORKFORTHEM

280.6 weissraum

280.7 weissraum

280.8 weissraum

280.9 310 K

280.10 310 K

280.1 Superlow

280.11 viagrafik

280.12 weissraum

280.13 bionic-systems

280.14 weissraum

281.1 WEWORKFORTHEM

281.2 WEWORKFORTHEM

281.3 WEWORKFORTHEM

281.4 weissraum

282.1 Unit Delta Plus

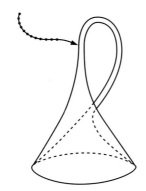

282.2 raster-noton

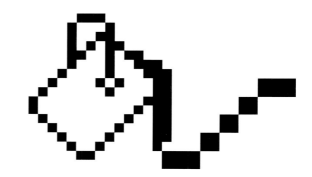

282.3 Syrup Helsinki

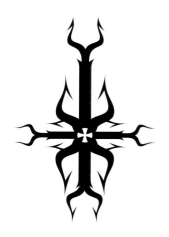

282.4 Superlow

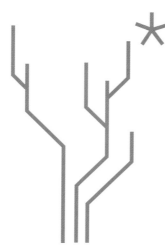

282.5 Raum Mannheim

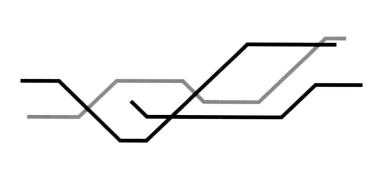

282.6 Raum Mannheim

CUÁNTICO
SUSTAINER

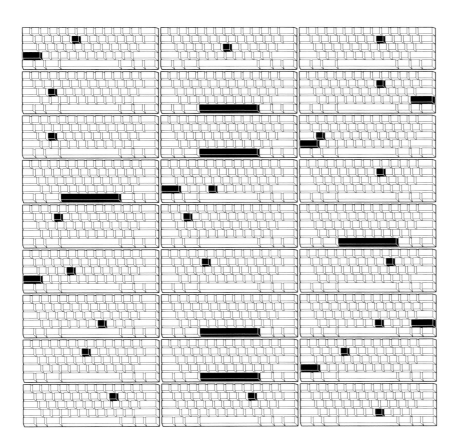

283.1 FLEAL

283.2 Andrea Krause

283.3 Andrea Krause

283.4 Andrea Krause

284.1 weissraum

284.2 weissraum

284.3 weissraum

284.4 weissraum

284.5 New Future People

284.6 weissraum

284.7 ZIP Design

284.8 Unit Delta Plus

284.9 stylodesign

284.10 Alexander Fuchs

284.11 OCKTAK

284.12 stylorouge

284.13 Jean-Jaques Tachdjian

284.14 Alexander Fuchs

284.15 A-Side Studio

284.16 Alexander Fuchs

285.1 Carsten Raffel   285.2 KEEP LEFT STUDIO   285.3 forcefeed:swede

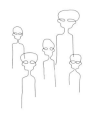

285.4 WEWORKFORTHEM   285.5 Happypets Products   285.6 Dubius?   285.7 incorect

285.8 Carsten Raffel   285.9 ZIP Design   285.10 Parra   285.11 KEEP LEFT STUDIO

286.1 struggle inc

286.2 Dubius?

286.3 weissraum

286.4 struggle inc

287.1 Angela Lorenz

288.1 Hort

288.2 Non-format

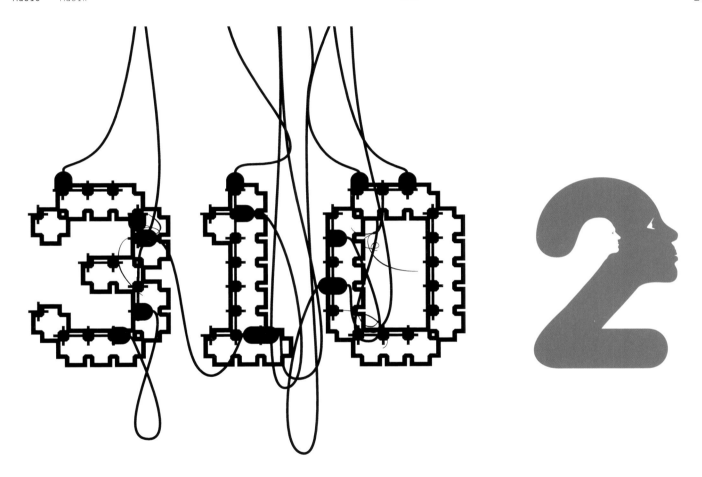

290.1 H5

290.2 Dubius?

290.3 no-domain

290.4 Nendo Graphic Squad

290.5 weissraum

290.6 Tsuyoshi Hirooka

290.7 Jürgen und ich

290.8 Superlow

290.9 INSECT

290.10 KEEP LEFT STUDIO

290.11 KEEP LEFT STUDIO

290.12 Masa Colectivo Gráfico

290.13 traum

290.14 Tsuyoshi Hirooka

290.15 Tsuyoshi Hirooka

290.16 Hugh Morse Design

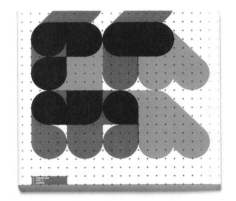

291.1 Hort

291.2 Carsten Raffel

291.3 J6Studios

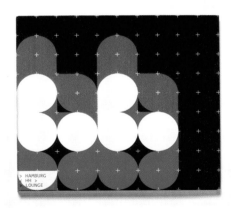

291.4 Hort

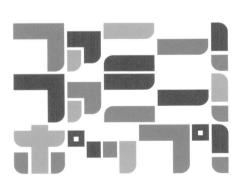

291.5 Maniackers Design

291.6 Carsten Raffel

292.1 no-domain

292.2 KEEP LEFT STUDIO

292.3 KEEP LEFT STUDIO

292.4 KEEP LEFT STUDIO

292.5 KEEP LEFT STUDIO

292.6 Parra

292.7 KEEP LEFT STUDIO

292.8 studiotonne

292.9 Jürgen und ich

292.10 nu designs+ yanku

292.11 bionic-systems

292.12 bleed

293.1 Zion Graphics

293.2 Kingsize

293.3 hirschindustries

293.4 bionic-systems

293.5 bleed

293.6 hirschindustries

293.7 INTEAM

293.8 Jürgen und ich

293.9 bleed

293.10 bleed

293.11 MetaDesign

293.12 Tsuyoshi Hirooka

293.13 doublestandards

293.14 ZIP Design

293.15 H5

293.16 Unit Delta Plus

294.1 310 K

294.2 BÜRO DESTRUCT

294.3 BÜRO DESTRUCT

294.4 Rinzen

294.5 KEEP LEFT STUDIO

294.6 stylodesign

294.7 KEEP LEFT STUDIO

294.8 WEWORKFORTHEM

294.9 52NORD

POWDERFINGER

295.1 Rinzen

STINA NORDENSTAM

295.2 Vår

295.3 bionic-systems

296.1 Jean-Jaques Tachdjian

296.2 bionic-systems

296.3 Rinzen

296.4 Rinzen

296.5 bleed

296.6 weissraum

296.7 bleed

297.1 bionic-systems

297.2 bionic-systems

297.3 bionic-systems

297.4 bionic-systems

297.5 bionic-systems

297.6 bionic-systems

297.7 ZIP Design

297.8 ZIP Design

298.1 bionic-systems

298.2 Unit Delta Plus

298.3 Oscar Reyes

298.4 KEEP LEFT STUDIO

URL: DRUMANDBASS.NO

298.5 bleed

298.6 bleed

299.1 Tsuyoshi Kusano

299.2 Nendo Graphic Squad

299.3 MK12 Design Studio

299.4 everyday icons

299.5 bionic-systems

299.6 BÜRO DESTRUCT

TEMPOVISION

299.7 H5

Logic Bomb™

299.8 bionic-systems

300.1 Karlssonwilker Inc.

300.2 weissraum

300.3 KEEP LEFT STUDIO

300.4 everyday icons

300.5 Hula Hula

300.6 ZIP Design

300.7 ZIP Design

300.8 Miguel Angel Leyva

300.9 Superlow

300.10 3 Particles

300.11 Zion Graphics

300.12 Jean-Jaques Tachdjian

300.13 Tsuyoshi Hirooka

300.14 studiotonne

300.15 Vår

300.16 Superlow

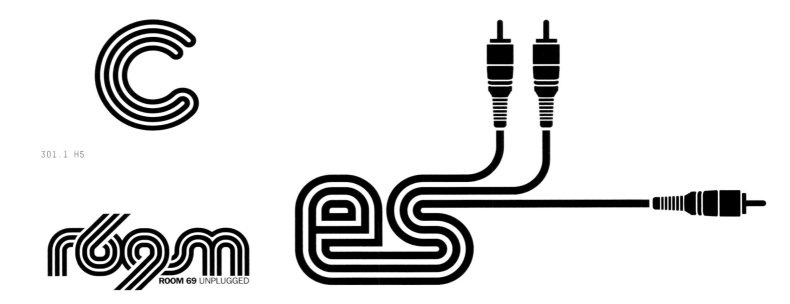

301.1 H5

301.2 viagrafik

301.3 no-domain

301.4 Hula Hula

301.5 St. Paulus Creative Force

302.1 bionic-systems

302.2 KEEP LEFT STUDIO

302.3 Masa Colectivo Gráfico

302.4 Nendo Graphic Squad

302.5 Maniackers Design

302.6 bionic-systems

302.7 Maniackers Design

302.8 Zion Graphics

302.9 viagrafik

303.1 Hula Hula

303.2 Hula Hula

303.3 Hula Hula

303.4 Hula Hula

303.5 Syrup Helsinki

303.6 A-Side Studio

303.7 Superlow

303.8 Hula Hula

303.9 studiotonne

303.10 Tsuyoshi Hirooka

303.11 Tsuyoshi Hirooka

303.12 310 K

303.13 Hula Hula

303.14 ZIP Design

303.15 Felix Braden

303.16 sub-static

304.1 inkgraphix

304.2 Jorge Alderete

304.3 Unit Delta Plus

304.4 Casarramona

304.5 Hula Hula

304.6 ZIP Design

304.7 inkgraphix

304.8 INSECT

305.1 Casarramona

305.2 Io Design

magnet

305.3 Unit Delta Plus

305.4 Hula Hula

electric blanket

305.5 Max Henschel

305.6 Unit Delta Plus

305.7 Jürgen und ich

305.8 bleed

306.1 Nonstop

306.2 Zion Graphics

306.3 weissraum

306.4 H5

306.5 Parra

306.6 Parra

306.7 inkgraphix

306.8 stylodesign

306.9 Tsuyoshi Hirooka

306.10 no-domain

306.11 no-domain

306.12 bionic-systems

306.13 inkgraphix

306.14 Vår

306.15 alphabetical order

306.16 Vår

307.1 eboy

307.2 eboy

307.3 Zion Graphics

307.4 viagrafik

307.5 Gianni Rossi

307.6 KEEP LEFT STUDIO

307.7 Tsuyoshi Hirooka

307.8 A-Side Studio

307.9 Zion Graphics

307.10 hirschindustries

307.11 KEEP LEFT STUDIO

307.12 KEEP LEFT STUDIO

307.13 wuff design

307.14 stylodesign

307.15 Um-bruch

307.16 KEEP LEFT STUDIO

308.1 Io Design

308.2 H5

308.3 Gianni Rossi

308.4 Unit Delta Plus

308.5 stylodesign

308.6 H5

309.1 doublestandards

310.1 doublestandards

310.2 doublestandards

310.3 wuff design

310.4 inkgraphix

310.5 Unit Delta Plus

310.6 inkgraphix

310.7 bleed

310.8 inkgraphix

310.9 Nobody

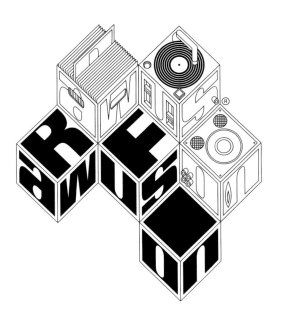

311.1 Vår

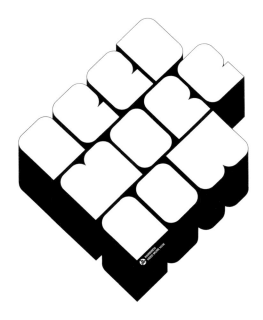

311.2 A-Side Studio

311.3 Karlssonwilker Inc.

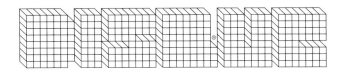

311.4 Vår

313.1 H5

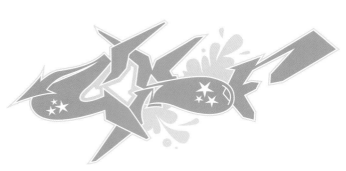

314.1 J6Studios

314.2 KEEP LEFT STUDIO

314.3 dmote

314.4 phunk

314.5 plumnotion

314.6 KEEP LEFT STUDIO

314.7 no-domain

314.8 no-domain

315.1 bionic-systems

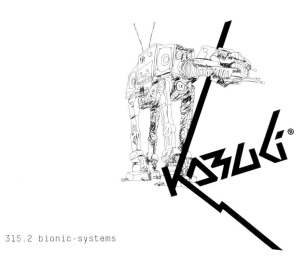

315.2 bionic-systems

315.3 KEEP LEFT STUDIO

315.4 bionic-systems

316.1 Hula Hula

316.2 Jürgen und ich

316.3 Masa Colectivo Gráfico

316.4 FROZT

316.5 Kingsize

316.6 viagrafik

316.7 New Future People

316.8 Zion Graphics

316.9 New Future People

316.10 New Future People

316.11 New Future People

316.12 New Future People

316.13 PFADFINDEREI

316.14 Nendo Graphic Squad

316.15 incorect

316.16 incorect

317.1 Factor Produkt

317.2 Factor Produkt

317.3 H5

317.4 H5

317.5 viagrafik

317.6 zorglob

317.7 viagrafik

317.8 H5

317.9 IKUILA

317.10 struggle inc

317.11 studiotonne

317.12 Zion Graphics

317.13 Tsuyoshi Hirooka

317.14 superfamous

317.15 weissraum

317.16 Zion Graphics

With Compliments

318.1 Parra

osito criminal RECORDS

318.2 Masa Colectivo Gráfico

MITTE·KARAOKE

318.3 Rikus Hilmann

CARRION CROW

318.4 INSECT

Los CACRi.

318.5 Masa Colectivo Gráfico

STOLEN

318.6 phunk

MACHINE

318.7 struggle inc

319.1 strange//attraktor

319.2 Carine Abraham

319.3 Gianni Rossi

319.4 Jorge Alderete

319.5 YipYop

319.6 the brainbox

319.7 Jorge Alderete

319.8 Jorge Alderete

320.1 hirschindustries

320.2 bleed

320.3 BlackJune

320.4 ZIP Design

320.5 weissraum

320.6 Unit Delta Plus

320.7 Masa Colectivo Gráfico

320.8 ZIP Design

320.9 Peter Vattanatham

320.10 YipYop

320.11 Masa Colectivo Gráfico

320.12 INSECT

321.1 traum

321.2 stylodesign

321.3 Unit Delta Plus

321.4 viagrafik

321.5 New Future People

321.6 Syrup Helsinki

321.7 hintze.gruppen

321.8 Masa Colectivo Gráfico

321.9 Casarramona

321.10 YipYop

321.11 Maniackers Design

321.12 Zion Graphics

321.13 ZIP Design

321.14 Raum Mannheim

321.15 MetaDesign

321.16 weissraum

322.1 Unit Delta Plus

322.2 Tsuyoshi Hirooka

322.3 blindresearch

322.4 Raum Mannheim

322.5 Masa Colectivo Gráfico

322.6 viagrafik

322.7 REGINA

322.8 Nendo Graphic Squad

322.9 superfamous

322.10 A-Side Studio

322.11 Raum Mannheim

322.12 Raum Mannheim

322.13 Nonstop

322.14 BÜRO DESTRUCT

322.15 Sebastian Gerbert

322.16 Factor Produkt

323.1 hintze.gruppen

323.2 zookeeper

323.3 OCKTAK

323.4 H5

323.5 traum

323.6 Tsuyoshi Hirooka

323.7 Jean-Jaques Tachdjiand

324.1 weissraum

324.2 Nonstop

324.3 Sanjai

324.4 no-domain

324.5 Jean-Jaques Tachdjian

324.6 zookeeper

324.7 stylodesign

324.8 Jürgen und ich

324.9 plumnotion

324.10 MK12 Design Studio

324.11 Felix Braden

324.12 Hausgrafik

324.13 studiotonne

324.14 New Future People

324.15 symbolodesign

324.16 weissraum

325.1 inkgraphix

325.2 Masa Colectivo Gráfico

325.3 Masa Colectivo Gráfico

325.4 Zion Graphics

325.5 Zion Graphics

325.6 forcefeed:swede

325.7 zookeeper

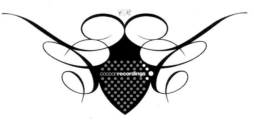

325.8 Surface

325.9 Tsuyoshi Hirooka

326.1 Masa Colectivo Gráfico

326.2 Unit Delta Plus

326.3 Io Design

326.4 Io Design

326.5 MK12 Design Studio

326.6 Unit Delta Plus

327.1 Tsuyoshi Hirooka

327.2 Pia Kolle

327.3 Kingsize

327.4 Gozer Media

327.5 plumnotion

327.6 weissraum

327.7 Superlow

327.8 struggle inc

327.9 Nendo Graphic Squad

328.1 Parra

328.2 Parra

328.3 BÜRO DESTRUCT

328.4 Karlssonwilker Inc.

329.1 Digitalultras

329.2 plumnotion

329.3 Hugh Morse Design

329.4 Hugh Morse Design

330.1 Unit Delta Plus

330.2 incorect

330.3 no-domain

330.4 plumnotion

330.5 J6Studios

330.6 Masa Colectivo Gráfico

331.1 INSECT

331.2 Parra

331.3 Parra

331.4 Parra

331.5 incorect

331.6 Maniackers Design

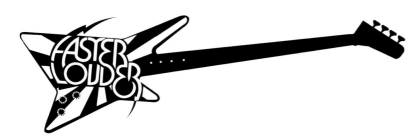

332.1 KEEP LEFT STUDIO

332.2 weissraum

332.3 Planet Pixel

332.4 Dubius?

332.5 KEEP LEFT STUDIO

332.6 KEEP LEFT STUDIO

332.7 weissraum

333.1 Angela Lorenz

333.2 Dubius?

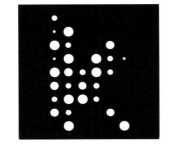

333.3 SCAPE

333.4 Zion Graphics

333.5 studiotonne

333.6 Masa Colectivo Gráfico

334.1 Parra

334.2 Gozer Media

334.3 Parra

334.4 incorect

334.5 310 K

335.1 310 K

335.2 PFADFINDEREI

335.3 weissraum

335.4 struggle inc

335.5 weissraum

335.6 Maniackers Design

335.7 Um-bruch

335.8 WEWORKFORTHEM

336.1 Planet Pixel

336.2 PFADFINDEREI

336.3 Raum Mannheim

336.4 bionic-systems

336.5 stylodesign

336.6 H5

336.7 bleed

336.8 FJD fujitajirodesign

336.9 viagrafik

336.10 sunrise studios

336.11 Propella

336.12 raster-noton

336.13 sub-static

336.14 traum

336.15 Norm

336.16 pictomat

337.1 Jorge Alderete

337.2 Jorge Alderete

337.3 INSECT

337.4 Gianni Rossi

337.5 Zion Graphics

337.6 A-Side Studio

337.7 symbolodesign

337.8 New Future People

337.9 Masa Colectivo Gráfico

337.10 plumnotion

337.11 Unit Delta Plus

337.12 ZIP Design

337.13 52NORD

337.14 a small percent

337.15 a small percent

337.16 bleed

338.1 WEWORKFORTHEM

338.2 viagrafik

338.3 viagrafik

338.4 viagrafik

338.5 viagrafik

338.6 viagrafik

339.1 Surface

339.2 Felix Braden

339.3 REGINA

339.4 alphabetical order

339.5 H5

339.6 Factor Produkt

339.7 BlackJune

339.8 Jürgen und ich

339.9 WEWORKFORTHEM

340.1 Casarramona

340.2 Casarramona

340.3 Gozer Media

340.4 Casarramona

340.5 Parra

340.6 Parra

340.7 Syrup Helsinki

340.8 Casarramona

340.9 Casarramona

341.1 alphabetical order

341.2 Masa Colectivo Gráfico

341.3 New Future People

341.4 Hula Hula

341.5 Carine Abraham

POLITICAL SOCIAL

POLITIK SOZIALES

How does the new designer scene deal with themes as different as political propaganda, events, protest demonstrations, charity projects and organisations, other NGOs, hospitals, social work? This chapter presents some current examples.

Wie setzt die neue Gestalterszene so unterschiedliche Themen wie politische Propaganda, Events, Protestmanifestationen, Wohltätigkeitsprojekte und – organisationen, andere NGOs, Spitäler oder Sozialarbeit um? Dieses Kapitel stellt aktuelle Beispiele dazu vor.

"J'AIME MES CLIENTS!"

Where do you get inspiration for your work?
What inspires us is mankind's lack of reason, perversion, war, communism, violence, nuclear weapons, sex, politics and television. Generally speaking we're more interested in ugliness and failure than beauty and correctness.

Do you work according to a definite design philosophy?
Yes, not like the majority of graphic halfwits in the early years of the new millennium who fell for a fashion that insisted on creating little crosses and clouds, polygons and pretty Mangas, constructing unusable 'floating' logos with illegible texts in two-point type. That gets to you! And because we don't work like that it leaves a whole virgin field free where we can romp around to our hearts' content. What I'd like to say to all these naïve little lambs, these peace-'n'-love graphic artists all over the world is: 'Keep it up, kids, you're on the right track. Good night!'

What would you say is the key to a good, successful logo?
No idea. We don't ask ourselves questions like that; we couldn't care less, to be honest. We don't really like logos; logos are for snobs and berks.

Do your aesthetic values and your clients' demands ever clash?
Sure they do! I can't see myself drawing a girl with a fat ruff for a bank, though ...

How do you resolve these clashes?
Quite simple: you go with the client; but OK, I admit, not everyone can love their clients. It's like this with us: the more demanding a difficult a client is, the more we love him. I'd even make a T-shirt with "I love my clients" on it.

If a client wasn't prepared to accept your work, how far would you be prepared to compromise?
We compromise and don't have any problem with preparing 2 or even 9587 versions for a client. But that doesn't happen very often, to our great regret. Clients aren't all that bad, you just have to be able to listen to them a bit and then you've got it, and it goes really well. I think it's arrogant and very easy too to get on a client's because he doesn't like the same colours as you, for example. We're all different, let's not forget that!

incorect, St. André, France | www.incorect.com

Wo holt ihr euch die Inspirationen für eure Arbeit?
Die Unvernunft der Menschheit, die Perversion, der Krieg, der Kommunismus, die Gewalt, die Nuklearwaffen, der Sex, die Politik und das Fernsehen. Ganz generell interessieren uns das Hässliche und die Versager mehr als das Schöne und die Korrekten.

Arbeitet ihr nach einer definierten Designphilosophie?
Ja, nicht wie die Mehrzahl jener unbedarften Grafiker, vor allem in den ersten Jahren des neuen Milleniums, einer Mode zu verfallen, in der es angesagt war, Polygone und niedliche Mangas zu kreieren, unbrauchbare Logos zu bauen, die ‚floaten', mit unlesbaren Texten in einer Zweipunktschrift. Das nervt! Und weil wir eben nicht auf dieser Schiene fahren, lässt das ein großes unbeackertes Feld frei, auf dem wir uns tummeln können. All diesen naiven Schäfchen, diesen Peace & Love-Grafikern rund um die Welt, möchte ich sagen: ‚Macht weiter so, Kinder, ihr seid auf dem richtigen Weg. Gute Nacht!'

Was charakterisiert in euren Augen ein gutes, ein gelungenes Logo?
Keine Ahnung. Wir stellen uns keine solchen Fragen; ehrlich gesagt ist uns das völlig egal. Wir lieben Logos nicht wirklich; Logos, das ist doch was für Snobs und Armleuchter.

Gibt's Konflikte zwischen euren ästhetischen Wertvorstellungen und den Ansprüchen eurer Kunden?
Ja, aber sicher! Ich sehe mich überhaupt nicht beim Zeichnen eines Mädchens mit einer dicken Halskrause für eine Bank, wobei...

Wie löst ihr solche Konflikte?
Ganz einfach: Man stellt sich auf den Kunden ein; aber okay, ich geb's zu, es ist nicht jedem gegeben, seine Kunden zu lieben. Bei uns ist es so: Je anspruchsvoller und schwieriger ein Kunde ist, desto mehr lieben wir ihn. Ich würde sogar ein T-Shirt mit dem Text „Ich liebe meine Kunden" machen.

Angenommen, ein Kunde akzeptiert eure Arbeit nicht: Wie weit lasst ihr euch dann auf Kompromisse ein?
Wir machen Kompromisse und haben null Probleme damit, 2 oder 9587 Versionen für einen Kunden anzufertigen. Kunden sind gar nicht so schlimm, man muss ihnen nur ein bisschen zuhören können, und dann hat man's auch schon kapiert, das läuft ganz gut. Ich find's ziemlich anmassend und auch zu einfach, einen Kunden unter dem Vorwand zu nerven , dass er nicht die gleichen Farben gut findet wie du zum Beispiel. Wir sind alle verschieden, vergessen wir das nicht!

incorect, St. André, Frankreich | www.incorect.com

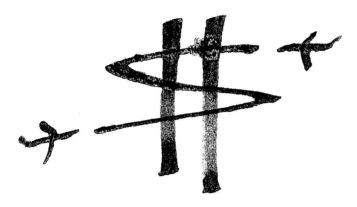

tower above terror

344.1 Ophorus

344.2 Martijn Oostra

344.3 incorect

344.4 HandGun

344.5 automatic art & design

344.6 Alexander Fuchs

344.7 Alexander Fuchs

344.8 Alexander Fuchs

344.9 Kong

344.10 Alexander Fuchs

344.11 Alexander Fuchs

BEWARE OF THE HAT! DON'T SIMPLIFY MEANING. PLEASE. ENJOY! *Politics*

345.1 wuff design

345.2 Superlow

345.3 Superlow

346.1 Io Design

346.2 viagrafik

346.3 viagrafik

346.4 Oscar Reyes

346.5 wuff design

346.6 wuff design

347.1 viagrafik

347.2 viagrafik

347.3 Kallegraphics

347.4 ohiogirl Design

347.5 viagrafik

347.6 wuff design

348.1 viagrafik

348.2 viagrafik

348.3 viagrafik

348.4 viagrafik

348.5 viagrafik

348.6 viagrafik

348.7 viagrafik

349.1 hirschindustries

349.2 viagrafik

349.3 wuff design

349.4 Masa Colectivo Gráfico

349.5 viagrafik

349.6 viagrafik

349.7 Masa Colectivo Gráfico

349.8 Masa Colectivo Gráfico

350.1 strange//attraktor

350.2 Kallegraphics

350.3 viagrafik

350.4 Unit Delta Plus

350.5 Unit Delta Plus

351.1 KEEP LEFT STUDIO

351.2 viagrafik

351.3 Karen Ingram

351.4 wuff design

351.5 viagrafik

352.1 Maniackers Design

352.2 struggle inc

352.3 Superlow

352.4 incorect

352.5 MetaDesign

352.6 fupete studio

knowledge

353.1 nu designs+ yanku

353.2 nu designs+ yanku

353.3 Dubius?

353.4 incorect

353.5 incorect

353.6 incorect

353.7 blindresearch

353.8 hirschindustries

353.9 viagrafik

354.1 zorglob

DEUTSCHER BUNDESTAG

354.2 Michael Thümmrich

connexion3d

354.3 moxi

STÓRIÐJUSKÓLINN

354.4 FROZT

All You Need Is
Teeth

354.5 polygraph

In Touch

354.6 Masa Colectivo Gráfico

Zilli
Mädchenstelle der kath. Kirche Biel

354.7 moxi

BASEMENT

354.8 Kallegraphics

s.a.r.a
SOCIETY

354.9 Meomi Design

SOILENT®
GREEN
ENGINEERED FOOD

354.10 viagrafik

méxico

354.11 Oscar Reyes

EAT YOUR
PETS
®

354.12 Superlow

IKEA
MUST
BURN

354.13 viagrafik

®

354.14 viagrafik

WE KNOW EVERYTHING

354.15 310 K

Therapiestelle für Kinder

355.1 Theres Steiner

355.2 a small percent

355.3 MetaDesign

355.4 Factor Produkt

355.5 Factor Produkt

355.6 FLASKAMP AG

355.7 a small percent

355.8 Moniteurs

355.9 Felix Braden

355.10 canefantasma studio

355.11 WEWORKFORTHEM

355.12 Judith Zaugg

355.13 Propella

ART, UNCLASSIFIABLE

KUNST, UNKLAS- SIERBARE ZEICHEN

There are interfaces between art and commerce: art quotes and imitates signs from the world of goods and vice versa. There are signs that ask us only to reflect and nothing else. There are signs that do not pursue any pragmatically designed purpose, but that still definitely 'make sense': because pleasure in experimentation makes sense as well. This chapter takes a look at exciting, provocative, and sometimes also absurd creations and exhibits from various experimental kitchens and studios.

Es gibt Schnittstellen zwischen Kunst und Kommerz: Kunst zitiert und imitiert Zeichen aus der Warenwelt und umgekehrt. Es gibt Zeichen, die ‚nur' zum Reflektieren auffordern und sonst gar nichts. Es gibt Zeichen, die sich keinem pragmatisch definierten Zweck zuordnen lassen, aber trotzdem keineswegs ‚sinnlos' sind: weil der Spaß am Experimentieren eben auch Sinn macht. Dieses Kapitel wirft einen Blick auf spannende, provokative, gelegentlich auch skurrile Kreationen und Exponate aus verschiedenen Experimentierküchen und Ateliers.

"FORM FOLLOWS DESIRE."

Where do you get inspiration for your work?
Pretty well everywhere.

Do you work according to a definite design philosophy?
Form follows desire – how about that?

What would you say is the key to a good, successful logo?
People should find it interesting even when it's detached from its function.

If it's true to say that works of art are now just goods whose provocative and disturbing elements no longer work in the spirit of the good old Enlightenment, but
are mere calculation in order to command the best possible price: how and where
would you place your own work? Or isn't it true to say that?
It wasn't true to say it even in the Enlightenment. The emergence of the book market, in
other words the fact that books are goods, played a pretty crucial part in the fact that
there even was something like the Enlightenment. Good works of art are "suitable" for
both enjoyment and criticism. It is just that things have got a bit more complicated as
everyone now knows that "provocative and disturbing elements" like superficial criticism
are good advertising material. Criticism will always be necessary as long as things have
to change. I am convinced that the "recipient" only responds positively to the elements
of a work that are addressed critically. For me that is the only way to meaningful re-
flection. Starting with the questions: why does that work and why are people going along
with it?

Wo findest du Inspirationen für deine Arbeit?
So ziemlich überall.

Arbeitest du nach einer definierten Designphilosophie?
Form follows desire – wie funktioniert das?

Was charakterisiert in deinen Augen ein gutes, ein gelungenes Logo?
Dass man es interessant findet, auch wenn man von seiner Funktion abstrahiert.

Falls die These stimmt, dass Kunstwerke nur noch Waren sind, deren provokative
und irritierende Elemente nichts mehr im Sinne der guten alten Aufklärung bewir-
ken, sondern reines Kalkül im Sinne einer Optimierung des Verkaufspreises sind:
Wie und wo würdest du dann deine Werke einordnen? Oder stimmt diese These
gar nicht?
Die These hat schon in der Aufklärung nicht gestimmt. Der entstehende Buchmarkt, also der Umstand, dass Bücher Waren sind, war ziemlich entscheidend dafür, dass es so
etwas wie Aufklärung überhaupt gegeben hat. Gute künstlerische Arbeiten sind sowohl
für den Genuss als auch für Kritik „geeignet". Nur dass sich das etwas verkompliziert
hat, da nun auch der Letzte weiß, dass „provokative und irritierende Elemente" wie
vordergründige Kritik ein gutes Werbemittel sind. Kritik wird immer notwendig sein, so-
lange sich was ändern muss. Die Frage ist nur, wie sie gestaltet wird. Ich setze darauf,
dass der „Rezipient" zuerst einmal das in der Rezeption einer Arbeit positiv erfährt, womit man sich kritisch auseinander setzt. Weil für mich nur so ein sinnvolles Nachdenken
möglich ist. Ausgehend von der Frage: Wieso läuft dass und wieso macht man auch mit?

Olaf Nicolai, Berlin, Germany | www.eigen-art.com

Olaf Nicolai, Berlin, Deutschland | www.eigen-art.com

358.1 Carsten Nicolai

358.2 Carsten Nicolai

358.3 Carsten Nicolai

Project description:
Work Index, page 438

Projektbeschreibung
Work Index, Seite 438

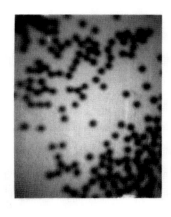

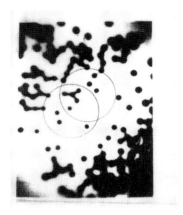

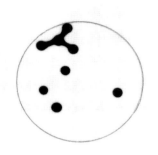

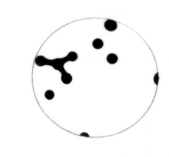

359.1 Carsten Nicolai   359.2 Carsten Nicolai   359.3 Carsten Nicolai   359.4 Carsten Nicolai

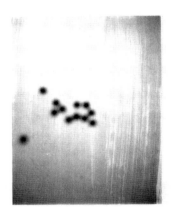

359.5 Carsten Nicolai   359.6 Carsten Nicolai   359.7 Carsten Nicolai

360.1 synchron

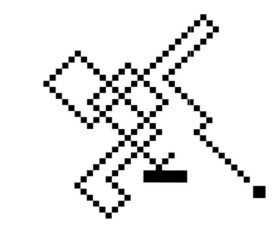

360.2 Tsuyoshi Hirooka

360.3 synchron

360.4 Tsuyoshi Kusano

Kaufhof Warehouse's façade, Dresden (DE)

361.1 Olaf Nicolai   361.2 Olaf Nicolai

362.1 Tsuyoshi Hirooka

362.2 Tsuyoshi Hirooka

362.3 Tsuyoshi Hirooka

362.4 viagrafik

362.5 Sebastian Gerbert

362.6 Tsuyoshi Hirooka

362.7 Tsuyoshi Hirooka

362.8 viagrafik

362.9 Tsuyoshi Kusano

362.10 Tsuyoshi Kusano

362.11 OCKTAK

362.12 polygraph

362.13 no-domain

362.14 no-domain

362.15 viagrafik

362.16 viagrafik

363.1 Tsuyoshi Hirooka

363.2 Tsuyoshi Hirooka

363.3 Tsuyoshi Hirooka

363.4 Tsuyoshi Hirooka

363.5 Tsuyoshi Hirooka

363.6 Tsuyoshi Hirooka

363.7 Tsuyoshi Hirooka

363.8 Tsuyoshi Hirooka

363.9 weissraum

363.10 weissraum

363.11 weissraum

363.12 polygraph

363.13 Tsuyoshi Hirooka

363.14 Tsuyoshi Hirooka

363.15 Tsuyoshi Hirooka

364.2 viagrafik

364.3 Tsuyoshi Hirooka

364.4 Carsten Raffel

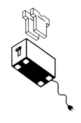

364.5 Tsuyoshi Hirooka

364.6 blindresearch

364.7 Alexander Fuchs

364.8 Tsuyoshi Kusano

364.9 weissraum

364.10 weissraum

364.1 Karlssonwilker Inc.

364.11 weissraum

364.12 jum

364.13 Parra

365.1 viagrafik

365.2 Parra

365.3 Parra

365.4 Parra

365.5 viagrafik

365.6 viagrafik

365.7 weissraum

365.8 no-domain

366.1 Parra

366.2 Parra

366.3 incorect

366.4 New Future People

367.1 viagrafik

367.2 viagrafik   367.3 viagrafik   367.4 viagrafik

368.1 incorect

368.2 incorect

368.3 incorect

368.4 incorect

368.5 Gianni Rossi

369.1 Tsuyoshi Hirooka

369.2 Tsuyoshi Hirooka

369.3 Guadamur

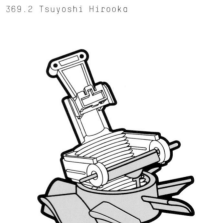

369.4 Tsuyoshi Hirooka

369.5 viagrafik

369.6 FLEAL

370.1 Tsuyoshi Hirooka

370.2 Tsuyoshi Hirooka

370.3 Tsuyoshi Hirooka

370.4 Tsuyoshi Hirooka

371.1 Tsuyoshi Hirooka   371.2 Tsuyoshi Hirooka   371.3 Maniackers Design

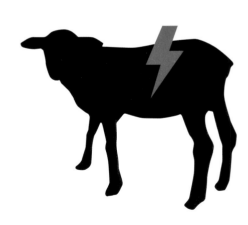

371.4 Tsuyoshi Kusano   371.5 Tsuyoshi Kusano

372.1 Guadamur   372.2 New Future People

373.1 Rebel One   373.2 Rebel One

374.1 Olaf Nicolai

375.1 Olaf Nicolai

376.1 fulguro

377.1 fulguro

378.1 SWEDEN

378.2 fulguro

378.3 fulguro

378.4 fulguro

379.1 baum magazin

379.2 baum magazin

379.3 baum magazin

379.4 baum magazin

380.1 strange//attraktor

380.2 polygraph

380.3 KEEP LEFT STUDIO

380.4 KEEP LEFT STUDIO

380.5 OCKTAK

380.6 blindresearch

GΠME

380.7 Tsuyoshi Hirooka

380.8 Tsuyoshi Hirooka

380.9 Sebastian Gerbert

380.10 Tsuyoshi Kusano

380.11 superfamous

380.12 BLU DESIGN

380.13 cubegrafik

380.14 Chris Hutchinson

380.15 Oscar Salinas Losada

380.16 Tsuyoshi Hirooka

381.1 Carsten Raffel   381.2 june

381.3 Tsuyoshi Hirooka

381.4 bleed

381.5 rubber type citizens

381.6 bleed

381.7 bleed

382.2 MAGNETOFONICA

382.3 Nendo Graphic Squad

382.4 Tsuyoshi Hirooka

382.5 Tsuyoshi Hirooka

382.6 Tsuyoshi Hirooka

382.7 polygraph

382.1 Tsuyoshi Hirooka

383.1 Deanne Cheuk

383.2 Deanne Cheuk

383.3 Deanne Cheuk

383.4 Deanne Cheuk

383.5 Deanne Cheuk

383.6 Deanne Cheuk

383.7 Deanne Cheuk

383.8 Deanne Cheuk

383.9 Deanne Cheuk

383.10 Deanne Cheuk

383.11 Deanne Cheuk

383.12 Deanne Cheuk

383.13 Deanne Cheuk

383.14 Deanne Cheuk

384.1 incorect

384.2 Parra

384.3 viagrafik

384.4 no-domain

384.5 WEWORKFORTHEM

385.1 everyday icons

385.2 Tsuyoshi Hirooka

385.3 june

385.4 Tsuyoshi Hirooka

385.5 june

386.1 FORK UNSTABLE MEDIA

386.2 incorect

386.3 Ministy of Information

386.4 no-domain

386.5 New Future People

386.6 a small percent

386.7 POWER GRAPHIXX

386.8 Tsuyoshi Hirooka

386.9 Tsuyoshi Hirooka

387.1 Olaf Nicolai

387.2 New Future People

387.3 viagrafik

387.4 viagrafik

388.1 sweaterweather

388.2 Chris Hutchinson

388.3 bleed

388.4 Parra

388.5 Parra

388.6 Parra

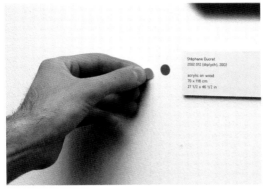

389.1 fulguro

389.2 fulguro

389.3 Raum Mannheim

389.4 Tsuyoshi Hirooka

389.5 PFADFINDEREI

389.6 june

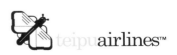

389.7 bleed

389.8 june

389.9 june

389.10 june

UV Ceti

390.1 Io Design

82 Eridani

390.2 Io Design

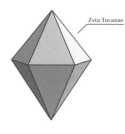

Zeta Tucanae

390.3 Io Design

Alpha Mensae

390.4 Io Design

391.1 nu designs+ yanku

SPORTS

SPORT

The world of sport, interpreted creatively and innovatively by design-ers: symbols for skateboards and supporters, for sports goods brands and sporting competitions.

Die Welt des Sports, von Gestaltern kreativ und innovativ interpre-tiert: Zeichen für Skateboard und Fans, für Sportartikelmarken und Wettkämpfe.

TOKIDOKI

"TO ME, BEING A DESIGNER IS NOT SO MUCH A PROFESSION AS A WAY OF LIFE."

Where do you get inspiration for your work?
I observe the world around me, I'm always on the lookout for inspiration. I don't find it in books, in magazines, on the Web, but in any normal phenomenon – someone just running past can inspire me with a good idea. The most important sources are for me are memories, dreams, everyday life, travel, and somehow there's always a link with Japan in there.

Do you work according to a definite design philosophy?
To me, being a designer is not so much a profession as a way of life. The best designers have a different view of reality from most other people. A designer observes, searches, stylises and makes things abstract, reflects, filters and transforms the things happening around him permanently in his head.

What would you say is the key to a good, successful logo?
As a general rule a logo ought to be powerful and substantial, essential and memorable. It should express what it stands for at a glance. The designer has to find something that is simple and yet unique. A quite unusual symbol can suit some clients or events – something like a mascot, a character, a special typeface. But it all depends on the media it's going to appear in and the particular situation.

Do your aesthetic values and your clients' demands ever clash?
It's normal for artists and businesspeople to be very different. It's my job to persuade them that my suggestion is the best way to achieve their aims. Art is a way of expressing your inner self, and communication is the way art is used as aesthetically as possible for the client's benefit.

If a client wasn't prepared to accept your work, how far would you be prepared to compromise?
I always try to find a creative solution that fits the client's style and needs. That's a question of professionalism. Not having satisfied a brief would be a personal defeat for me.

Wo holst du dir die Inspirationen für deine Arbeit?
Ich beobachte die Welt um mich herum, immer auf der Suche nach Inspirationen. Die finde ich nicht in Büchern, in Magazinen, im Web, sondern in jeder ganz normalen Erscheinung – sogar jemand, der einfach nur vorbei läuft, kann mich zu einer guten Idee inspirieren. Die wichtigsten Quellen für mich sind Erinnerungen, Träume, der Alltag... Reisen, und immer ist irgendein Bezug zu Japan dabei.

Arbeitest du nach einer definierten Designphilosophie?
Für mich ist Designer sein nicht so sehr ein Beruf sondern eine Lebensart. Die besten Designer betrachten die Realität aus einer anderen Perspektive als die meisten anderen Menschen. Ein Gestalter beobachtet, sucht, stilisiert und abstrahiert, denkt nach, filtert und transformiert in seinem Kopf permanent die Dinge, die um ihn herum passieren.

Was charakterisiert in deinen Augen ein gutes, ein gelungenes Logo?
Als generelle Regel sollte das ideale Logo kräftig und gehaltvoll sein, essentiell und einprägsam. Es sollte auf einen Blick das ausdrücken, wofür es steht. Der Gestalter muss nach etwas suchen, das einfach und trotzdem einzigartig ist. Für manche Kunden oder Events kann ein eher ausgefallenes Zeichen passen – wie etwa ein Maskottchen, ein Charakter, eine spezielle Schrift. Doch das hängt von den Medien ab, in denen es erscheint, und von der jeweiligen Situation.

Gibt's Konflikte zwischen deinen ästhetischen Wertvorstellungen und den Ansprüchen deiner Kunden?
Es ist normal, dass Künstler und Geschäftsleute sehr verschiedene Leute sind. Es ist mein Job sie zu überzeugen, dass mein Vorschlag der beste Weg zum Erreichen ihrer Ziele ist. Kunst ist die Art, sein inneres Selbst auszudrücken, und Kommunikation ist die Art, Kunst auf möglichst ästhetische Weise zum Nutzen seines Kunden anzuwenden.

Angenommen, ein Kunde akzeptiert deine Arbeit nicht: Wie weit lässt du dich dann auf Kompromisse ein?
Ich versuche immer die kreative Lösung zu finden, die dem Stil und den Ansprüchen des Kunden entspricht. Das ist eine Frage der Professionalität. Einen Auftrag nicht erfüllt zu haben wäre für mich eine persönliche Niederlage.

Tokidoki, Rome, Italy | www.tokidoki.it

Tokidoki, Rom, Italien | www.tokidoki.it

394.1 Tsuyoshi Hirooka

394.2 J6Studios

394.3 Carsten Raffel

394.4 jum

394.5 jum

394.6 Alexander Fuchs

395.1 BlackJune

395.2 TOKIDO

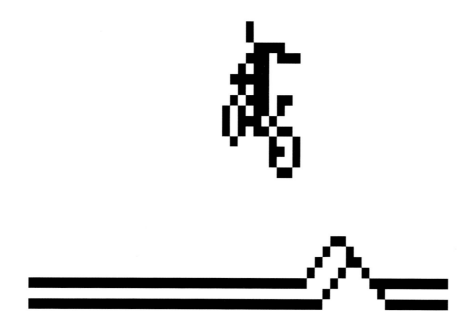

396.1 Nendo Graphic Squad

396.2 310 K

396.3 Mark Sloan

396.4 jum

SIZE DOESN'T MATTER

397.1 jum   397.2 TOKIDO   397.3 310 K

398.1 A-Side Studio

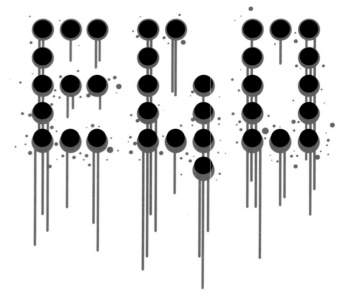

398.2 Carsten Raffel

398.3 Dubius?

398.4 viagrafik   398.5 HandGun

399.1 bionic-systems

399.2 J6Studios

399.3 a small percent

399.4 Max Henschel

399.5 tokidoki

399.6 zookeeper

399.7 weissraum

399.8 tokidoki

399.9 J6Studios

400.1 struggle inc

400.2 Max Henschel

400.3 Sebastian Gerbert

400.4 GWG CO. LTD

400.5 Casarramona

400.6 Casarramona

400.7 Casarramona

400.8 Unit Delta Plus

400.9 zookeeper

400.10 Max Henschel

400.11 J6Studios

400.12 Max Henschel

400.13 Carsten Raffel

400.14 Carsten Raffel

400.15 tokidoki

400.16 strange//attraktor

401.1 HandGun

401.2 HandGun

401.3 Max Henschel

401.4 plumnotion

401.5 New Future People

401.6 tokidoki

401.7 tokidoki

401.8 J6Studios

401.9 typotherapy

401.10 ZIP Design

401.11 zookeeper

401.12 zookeeper

401.13 BÜRO DESTRUCT

401.14 weissraum

401.15 Kallegraphics

401.16 Kallegraphics

402.1 ohiogirl Design

402.2 polygraph

402.3 Casarramona

402.4 Casarramona

403.1 fupete studio

ADDRESS INDEX

WORK INDEX

Project description
random.logo.dot
Carsten Nicolai, 1999

/: courtesy:
Galerie EIGEN+ART Berlin

Figure: page 358

Projektbeschreibung
random.logo.dot
Carsten Nicolai, 1999

/: courtesy:
Galerie EIGEN+ART Berlin

Abbildung: Seite 358

The basis of the design is photographic footage on a membrane moveable steel ball. The oscillation of the membrane is created through ground noise and keeps the balls moving. The photographic footage allows optical deformations anc chance patterns to form as a result of the camera shake.

Regions are choosen from these chance patterns, copies are enlarged and clear contourdrawing are prepared. These clear point constellations form the new basic identity of the logo for the Frankfurter Kunstverein.

Designbasis: Fotos, die durch eine an einer Lautsprechermembrane ange-brachte bewegliche Stahlkugel generiert werden. Die Bewegungen der Membrane werden durch Geräusche erzeugt und halten die Kugeln in Bewegung. Eine Ka-mera nimmt die Bewegungen auf. Die Fotos sind optische Deformationen und zufällige Formen.

Aus den entstandenen Formen werden Ausschnitte ausgewählt, kopiert, und vergrössert, klare Umrisse werden de-finiert: Aus diesen, auf den Punkt ge-brachten Konstellationen entsteht die Basisidentität des neuen Logos für den Frankfurter Kunstverein.

STATISTICS

STATISTICS

STATISTIKEN

This table of elements on page 440 shows the basic components used to construct a logo. Neither the design technique (Vector graphics, sketch, etc.) nor form (abstract, pictographic, iconographic, ideographic, illustrative) are included because they do not directly affect the form of the logo.

The table of combinations on page 441 shows how logos can be constructed from up to three basic elements. All further combinations are summarized under the term complex combinations (fusion) and are not listed here.

Die Tabelle der Elemente auf Seite 440 zeigt die elementaren Komponenten, aus den ein Logo konstruiert wird. Die Darstellungstechnik (Vektorgrafik, Handskizze, usw.) sowie die Darstellungsart (abstrakt, piktografisch, ikonografisch, ideografisch, illustrativ) sind dabei nicht berücksichtigt, weil sie keinen direkten Einfluss auf die Form des Logos haben.

Die Tabelle der Kombinationen auf Seite 441 zeigt, wie aus bis zu 3 Grundelementen Logos konstruiert werden können. Alle weiteren Kombinationen sind unter dem Begriff Komplexe Kombinationen (Verschmelzungen) zusammengefasst und hier nicht aufgelistet.

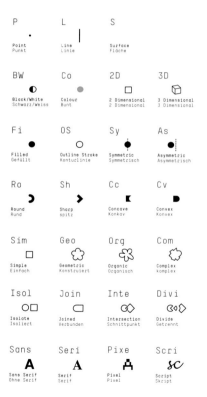

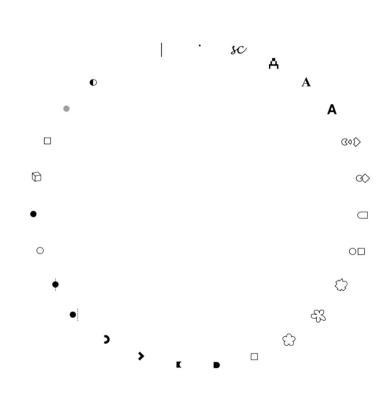

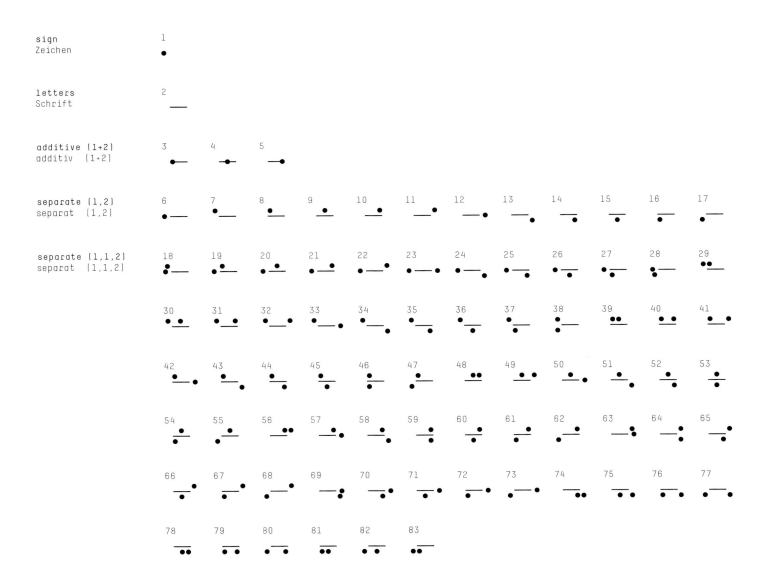

sign
Zeichen

letters
Schrift

additive (1+2)
additiv (1+2)

separate (1,2)
separat (1,2)

separate (1,1,2)
separat (1,1,2)

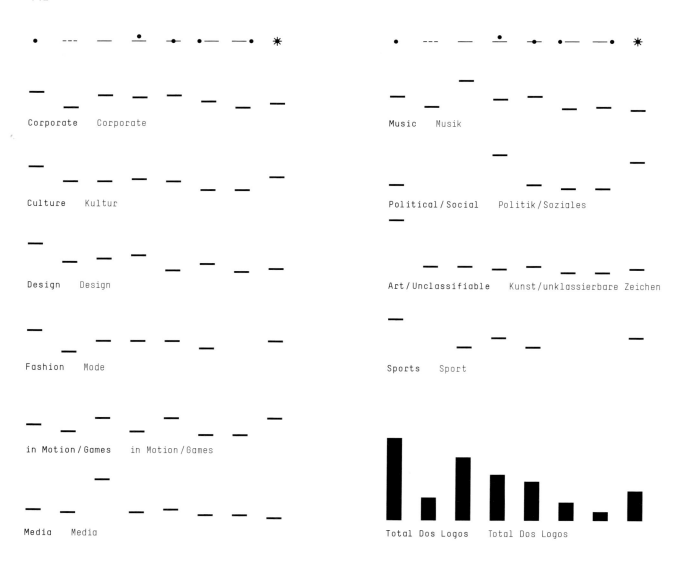

Corporate   Corporate

Culture   Kultur

Design   Design

Fashion   Mode

in Motion/Games   in Motion/Games

Media   Media

Music   Musik

Political/Social   Politik/Soziales

Art/Unclassifiable   Kunst/unklassierbare Zeichen

Sports   Sport

Total Dos Logos   Total Dos Logos

A Selected Logo Collection

Edited by Robert Klanten, Nicolas Bourquin
Layout and Design by Nicolas Bourquin, www.onlab.ch
Design assistance and index management by Matthias Hübner
Fontdesign T-Star Mono Rounded by Mika Mischler, www.binnenland.ch
Logo, cover design and statistics by Nicolas Bourquin

Prologue and Essay by Roland Müller
Interviews by Nicolas Bourquin and Roland Müller
Translated by Michael Robinson and Junko Tozaki
Proof-Reading by Textra Berlin and Sonja Commentz

Production management by Janni Milstrey
Production assistance by Vinzenz Geppert, Gunhild Hänsch, Martina Walter

Editorial support Japan by Junko Tozaki

Published by Die Gestalten Verlag, Berlin
Printed by Offsetdruckerei Karl Grammlich GmbH
Made in Germany

6th printing, 2007   351097

Bibliographic information published by the Deutsche Nationalbibliothek
The Deutsche Nationalbibliothek lists this publication in the Deutsche
Nationalbibliografie; detailed bibliographic data are available in the Internet
at http://dnb.d-nb.de.

ISBN 978-3-89955-055-9

For your local dgv distributor please check out:
www.die-gestalten.de